Oklahoma State University's

School of International Studies

A History of Leadership & Learning

By Paul William Bass & Katie Sewell

NEW FORUMS

NEW FORUMS PRESS INC.

Published in the United States of America
by New Forums Press, Inc.1018 S. Lewis St.
Stillwater, OK 74074
www.newforums.com

Library of Congress Cataloging-in-Publication Data Pending

This book may be ordered in bulk quantities at discount from New Forums Press, Inc., P.O. Box 876, Stillwater, OK 74076 [Federal I.D. No. 73 1123239]. Printed in the United States of America.

ISBN 10: 1-58107-262-7
ISBN 13: 978-1-58107-262-4

.

Table of Contents

Dedication

A common factor expressed in the creation of the School of International Studies (SIS), the development of the SIS, and the stability of the SIS, during the first decade of existence, has been the presence and activity of one individual, Dr. James Hromas. Through interviews and research of extensive files, Dr. James Hromas was an active participant. Students interviewed attribute great praise and appreciation for his leadership and personal assistance.

Dr. Hromas passed away on Oct. 12, 2015 and in honor for his significant contributions to the SIS the author has taken the privilege of dedicating this book to him.

December 16, 1944 – October 12, 2015

Dr. James Hromas

Retired Director, School of International Studies
Oklahoma State University

Authors' Notes

This was a challenging, but enjoyable book to write. The three earlier books in the Bennett Centennial Series were centered around a personality- Henry Garland Bennett. Over a period of five years I was able to grow in my appreciation for the man, his family and the institution that he so loved- Oklahoma A & M College. This book is centered around an important part of that institution, now Oklahoma State University, that carries on the legacy of Bennett through international education. In researching for the three earlier books, many trips were necessary to discover resources and find family members. For this book, I was fortunate to have a centralized file at OSU and university personnel readily available for interviews. It was more challenging to write a book about an institutional program than an individual. Writing a book about an individual is an attempt to discover the many aspects of one individual personality. Institutional program development involves a collection of professional personalities that are needed to cooperate in achieving goals.

Another challenge in writing this book was the original motivation in starting the process. The three Bennett Centennial Series books were self-started by my own interest and curiosity. I was honored to be commissioned by the Oklahoma State University School of International Studies to undertake this project. Answering to an institution and writing primarily for an academic audience is much more challenging. Self-motivation is still an important part of both processes.

Another challenge in writing this book was the sensitivity to academic institutional politics. Every university department has its historical battles for power, funding and protectionism. A university program of this scope also encounters such conflicts and struggles. In writing about an individual such as Bennett, one also has to consider those few negative experiences in an honest but tactful manner in consideration of the family. It is my desire to try and record honestly but tactfully the record of those few institutional conflicts.

There were several advantages in writing this type of book. One advantage was familiarity with the School of International Studies staff. During the experience of writing the earlier three books in the Bennett series, the SIS staff was very encouraging and helpful. In addition to the purchase of numerous books for their public relations efforts, they also included me as a part of their many scheduled activities including award banquets and milestone celebrations. Over the course of the last several years my personal relationship with the staff has expanded beyond being professional to include genuine friendships.

Another advantage in writing this book was the centralization of research resources. The SIS staff worked hard to create a central collection area of pertinent files and materials. These numerous papers and booklets were well organized and easily accessible. Personal interviews were mostly located around Stillwater and Oklahoma City. In the previous works many hours were spent traveling across four states and researching unfamiliar files and conducting individual interviews.

A final advantage was my personal interest and appreciation for the School of International Studies. It is a modern-day connection to the life's work of Henry Garland Bennett on the very location of his long-term tenure as president of what he knew as Oklahoma A & M College. He was the inspiration for the school's international development and serves as the standard for academic and practical application of international interests.

It is my hope that this book will link the significance of the Bennett years to the current and future understanding and appreciation for the Oklahoma State University's School of International Studies.

Introduction

Oklahoma A & M President Henry Garland Bennett made special trips to countries in South America, Europe, the Near East, northern Africa and the Far East. Those early encounters led to over half a century of direct university involvement in international education and outreach that included administration, faculty and students. Fifteen years ago, that international involvement found academic and practical application through the founding of the School of International Studies at Oklahoma State University.

Oklahoma State University President Burns Hargis has renewed and expanded the international mission of OSU in a stronger way than any President since Henry Bennett. President Hargis has utilized the relationship building tool of a Presidential visit to stimulate OSU's international connections in Turkey (July 2010), China (June 2011), Brazil (June 2012), England, India (March 2013) and Mexico (January 2014).

OSU President Burns Hargis and Ann Hargis are pictured with Dr. José Alfredo Miranda López and his wife, Maria. Dr. Miranda is the past president of UPAEP University located in Puebla City, Mexico.

During his visit to China in June 2011, President Hargis visited China Agricultural University in Beijing, Southwest Jiatong University and Southwest University of Finance and Economics in Chengdu (plus several other Chinese institutions of higher learning). These University visits supported stronger relationships that produced increases in both graduate and undergraduate Chinese student enrollment at OSU, as well as visiting scholar exchanges and a strengthening of OSU's Chinese language offerings. Mr. Tim Huff, Director of the Office of International Students and Scholars and Ms. Vivian Wang, also of ISS, assisted in the development of the visit to China.

During a visit to India, President Hargis was helped immensely by Mr. Lakshmaiah Ponnala, Honorable Minister of Information Technology and Communications, Government of Andhra Pradesh, India and Mr. MVL Prasad, a successful businessman and entrepreneur from the Dallas, Texas area. Together, these OSU alums provided access to many institutions of higher education and technology in India.

President Hargis has also encouraged students at OSU to embrace internationalization. He personally requested that the Greek system lead by altering their pledge system to make it possible for international students to enter fraternities and sororities. While this may not impact a large number of students, the message of acceptance and support for diversity that it sends will transcend the campus.

President V. Burns Hargis and First Cowgirl Ann Hargis have given selflessly of their time by attending a wide variety of events sponsored by International Student Organizations on campus. These include the International Bazaar, Diwali Night and other events where international students share their culture and heritage. President Hargis has written editorial letters that have been published statewide encouraging internationalization and study abroad programs. He has been a tireless supporter of OSU's Division of International Studies and Outreach and is leading OSU in the right direction for the future of the University.

Any credible educational institution is first and foremost about people. Qualified teachers lead eager students to absorb information that will improve their lives and the lives of others. Such is the case with the OSU's School of International Studies. The program uniquely combines the efforts to educate international students in an advanced degree program as well as to educate domestic students in international affairs. Two individual examples are presented. One is an international student coming to OSU for an education. The other is an Oklahoma student discovering the world through OSU.

Diego Alvarez came to OSU from Colombia, South America. He was one of the early participants in the SIS and graduated in September 2001. He worked for the United Nations Office on Drugs and Crime in Colombia for five years. He then was able to work with the United Nations International Commission against Impunity in Guatemala. During this same period after graduation, Diego was also able to take advantage of numerous travel opportunities to international conferences. In Israel he attended a conference that was a workshop on media strategies for social change; in Spain he attended a conference on international cooperation and in Nairobi he helped with a conference on communications strategy. He has also made several trips to the commission headquarters in Vienna. His experiences at the OSU SIS prepared him academically and culturally for the demands of his chosen profession.[1]

Kathleen (Kat) Furr is an Oklahoman from Tulsa with a family legacy of OSU graduates. She was raised overseas in Dharan, Saudia Arabia. She completed her undergraduate work at OSU in political science and Furr had a career desire for Middle Eastern studies. After exploring the options for an advanced degree, she was happy to discover that the OSU SIS offered the best plan for a master's degree program. The SIS not only provided that academic certification but actually led to her career employment. She received a paid four month internship at the Zayed University in Dubai, United Arab Emirates at the Economic & Policy Research Unit. She graduated from the SIS in May 2009 and was hired to continue her work at Zayed University at the National Research Foundation. Furr credits her experiences at SIS with sharpening her awareness of cultural differences. Her experiences with the OSU Student Association of Global Affairs (SAGA) taught her leadership, event planning and appreciation for cultural differences. She is anxious for the SIS to develop a doctoral program opportunity. Kat said that "There is nowhere in the world I can go now and feel alone. The friends I made are global and we share a bond as SIS family, on which I can count anytime I need a hand."[2]

The uniqueness of the School of International Studies at OSU is the combination of disciplines of academic study with international experiences. Many schools may offer the opportunity for some international experience in travel and short-term study. But few schools offer the opportunity for an accredited program of international study on a master's degree level. OSU's history of international involvement is presented along with the creation and development of the School of International Studies. It is important to look beyond the factual data and historical information to see the real impact on the lives of people. Many stories are presented of real people who have experienced the OSU international studies programs and are making an impact on a global level.

It is important to recognize the contributions of OSU alum Jerry Gill who has chronicled in much more detail the history of the international programs at OSU from the time of Henry Bennett to 1990. His books, *The Great Adventure* (1978) and *International Programs, Centennial Series* (1991), are standards in understanding the record of the campus' international involvement. This book looks at the international connections with Oklahoma A & M before Henry Bennett, gives a summary of the international work on campus from Bennett to 1990, then expands the creation and development of the School of International Studies.[3]

The three sections of this book are important in an understanding of the OSU School of International Studies. *Legacy and Leadership* are important because of the foundational standard laid by dedicated people with vision far beyond their immediate activities. *Leading and Learning are* also important because of the ongoing availability of committed leaders among the faculty and administration of OSU. *Learning and Looking* are vitally important because of the goals, measurement and direction of academically-oriented programs. The three sections come together in a basic understanding of what the OSU School of International Studies encompasses.

Foreword

V. Burns Hargis, President, Oklahoma State University
December 2013

Oklahoma State University has a proud legacy as one of America's premier land-grant universities. Through its mission of teaching, research and outreach the school has not only served the people of Oklahoma with distinction, but has shared its talent and expertise with people around the world. OSU is truly a global university.

As 18th president of this outstanding university, I serve in humble admiration of OSU President Henry Bennett. It is safe to say that Dr. Bennett is the father of the OSU we know today. His vision for campus facilities and architecture, his focus on student access and his commitment to our land-grant mission throughout the world moved OSU forward by leaps and bounds.

Of all his accomplishments, OSU's international outreach may be Henry Bennett's greatest legacy. He put Oklahoma State University on the world map. From the beginning, OSU has welcomed international students to its campus, the first foreign student enrolled in 1899. But it was through Dr. Bennett's inspiration and leadership that OSU looked far beyond the horizon and took outreach to another level. At the same time, the university opened its arms to students from all points on the globe. Today OSU has students from more than 110 countries, or more than half the countries in the world. Through this two-way international expansion, Dr. Bennett taught us the valuable lesson of mutual learning.

In *Leadership and Learning*, author Paul Bass has taken on the important and interesting task of chronicling the history of Oklahoma State University's international journey. The author's thorough research and thoughtful insight offer a glimpse at the people and events that paved the way for the formation of the OSU School of International Studies. Mr. Bass also lays out the challenges and offers his thoughts on what OSU must do to not only carry on its international mission, but to achieve even greater success at home and abroad.

In today's shrinking world and global economy, an understanding and appreciation of those beyond our own borders is critical to the future success and harmony of our world. I am committed to greater international involvement for our students, increased opportunities for international students on our campus, and expanding Oklahoma State University's reach throughout the world.

This book explores the involvement and impact of many in OSU's international voyage. I want to acknowledge Wes and Lou Watkins, whose generosity helped create the Wes Watkins Center for International Trade and Development, as well as the Wes Watkins Distinguished Lectureship program. OSU Presidents Oliver Willham, Robert Kamm, Lawrence Boger, James Halligan and David Schmidly kept the vision of Henry Bennett alive. There are many others who played influential roles. We honor and thank them all. I know you will enjoy reading about them.

OSU President Burns Hargis

OSU International Activity Time Line

Prior to the School of International Studies

1899 First international student enrolled
1931 Bennett toured Europe for Rotary Club
1946 Bennett served in Quebec
1949 Bennett served in Germany
      Newman Club established scholarship program for
      "foreign" students
1950 Bennett served in Ethiopia
      Bennett selected as Point Four director
1951 Office of International Programs
      First international project in Ethiopia (1952-1968)
1955 Project in Pakistan (1955-1970)
1968 Project in Thailand (1968-1973)
1969 Reader's Digest Award
1970 English Language Institute established at OSU
1971 Project in Egypt
1980 Project in Jordan (1981-1984)
1984 Center for International Trade Development established
1987 Project in Kameoka
1991 Project in Japan (1991-1995)
1994 Project in Kazakhstan (1994 - 2002)
1996 Study Abroad Office
1998 Approval by Board of Regents
1999 Dedication Ceremony
      Fiftieth anniversary of Point Four
2001 Wes Watkins Distinguished Lectureship program revamped
2002 Lawrence L. Boger Distinguished Graduate Fellowship
      awarded

Wes Watkins Center International Plaza ground breaking
2003 Reciprocal agreements with three Mexican universities
Wes and Lou Watkins establish three graduate fellowships
2004 Phi Beta Delta chapter chartered
Project in Iraq (2004-2006)
2008 Dedication of the Lou Watkins International Courtyard
2009 Tenth anniversary ceremony
Dedicational of the International Mall and Flag Courtyard
Wes Watkins International Plaza Dedication
2010 Dr. James Hromas retirement
Transition Period
2011 Dr. David Henneberry leadership
"Point Four" films- Mel Tewahade
Cathey and Donald Humphreys study abroad scholarships
2012 "Allegro" musical show
Hosting former British Prime Minister Tony Blair and
former Secretary of Defense Robert Gates
National Guard correspondence and training
Wes Watkins Center for International Trade Development
staff
2013 Dr. James Hromas receives Bennett Fellow award
2014 Jim Clifton receives Bennett Fellow award
2015 Brothers, Jalal Farzaneh and Mohammad Farzaneh gift
$1.6 million to Oklahoma State University to begin
Iranian and Persian Gulf Studies at OSU

Photo Index

Part One:
Legacy and Leadership

"The vision which formed the foundation for the School of International Studies reflects Dr. Boger's dedication to extending the legacy of international education at Oklahoma State University."
(Dr. Robert L. Sandmeyer, Former Dean, College of Business Administration, Dr. Lawrence L. Boger Distinguished Professorships brochure, 2000)

"Capitalizing on our legacy in international education, the School of International Studies will unite our international resources to enhance programs and services for the global community."
(President James E. Halligan, Dedication Service, April 1, 1999)

The First Forty Years (1890-1928)

The university at Stillwater is unique in many ways. It is unique in its founding, its purpose and its relationships. It was founded before Oklahoma became a state. It was established as a land-grant college. It was a leader in international relationships.

The College's Founding

The college had its founding in a location considered as a foreign culture- American Indian Territory. The 1889 Oklahoma Land Rush created settlements and towns in the undeveloped area.

Signs as you enter Stillwater say, "Where Oklahoma began." The Oklahoma Territory was established in 1890. That same year the college was established as a land-grant school. With the amended Morrill Act of 1890 and the established Oklahoma and Indian Territories, the college found itself in a strategic place with a single purpose. The land-grant schools were established by each state for the purpose of instruction with "such branches of learning as are related to agriculture and the mechanical arts in such a manner as the legislature of the state might prescribe in order to promote the liberal and practical education of the industrial classes in the several pursuits and professions of life." These and other provisions were accepted by the enacted Constitution of Oklahoma (Article II, Section 1). Additional agreements included instructions in the English language, the various branches of math, physical, natural and economic sciences. Acceptance of the 1887 Hatch Act required creation of "a state experiment station which would be used for agricultural research, the results of which would be disseminated to farmers and ranchers throughout Oklahoma and the nation."[1] Sixty years later the college's instruction and experiment stations would find their way across oceans to international lands.

The first president of the Oklahoma Agricultural and Mechanical College was Robert Barker, who served from 1891 until 1894. He organized the college into academic departments and led in recruitment. Ironically, he was "rewarded" in the heavily Democratic Oklahoma by being dismissed for his Republican leanings.[2] This was a hint of the struggle for the Oklahoma A & M's leadership for the first forty years.

Education and State Politics

As a land-grant school, oversight was through the State Department of Agriculture's Board of Regents. The politically-appointed board was controlled by the governor and the state legislature. The college itself had very little autonomy in practices, including hiring and firing. Oklahoma A & M's presidents served at the desires and whims of the board. In the first thirty-seven years there were ten presidents with an average tenure of 3.7 years. Angelo C. Scott served as president form 1899 until 1908- a nine-year term.[3] It was during his term that there was the greatest expansion of enrollment and college productivity. The college suffered greatly in its potential growth because of the political infighting and lack of faculty tenure. With the arrival of Henry Garland Bennett the college would see major progress, a lessening of political control, the development of tenure for faculty and the formation of the Oklahoma State Regents for Higher Education.

Foreign Students

Some think that there was little, if any, international involvement with the college before the arrival of Henry Bennett. There was actually early and significant international presence. The first international student was Avedis G. Adjemian, who was enrolled in 1899.[4] The 1906-07 Redskins Yearbook recorded a "Sub Freshman," Forest Baker, from Manila, Philippine Islands. At the end of President Scott's term it was recorded that "young men and women from Illinois, Indian Territory, Indiana, Iowa, Kansas, Missouri, New Mexico, North Carolina, Oklahoma Territory, Pennsylvania, and one foreign country attended the A. and M. College." The 1910-11 Redskins Yearbook recorded second year students Henry Heierding from Stadthagen, Germany, and William Mardon from Wiesbaden, Germany.[5]

The number of international students increased to such a point that in 1921 the college established an International Relations Club for the purpose of "increasing world understanding among faculty and students." In 1922 the club was nationalized as the Cosmopolitan Club with the purpose to "bring about a better understanding between the students of the United States and foreign countries." This understanding was to be "political, social, economic and commercial." By 1926 the Cosmopolitan Club had students from Argentina, Guam, the Philippines, Canada and Egypt.[6]

Although the international involvement of the college was limited in comparison to the next several decades, many factors brought the world to the small college. The outbreak of World War I saw many students and families affected by activities in foreign countries. Many refugee families came to the United States with hopes for a better life for their children through higher education. Even though the United States would drift back to a foreign policy of isolationism, the impact of exposure to the world through the war could not be forgotten.

The Bennett Years (1928-1951)

Henry Garland Bennett was born four years before the college in Stillwater was founded. He was raised with positive personal values, a strong work ethic and a recognition of the importance of a good education.

Bennett's Background

Born in rural, south Arkansas in December 1886, Henry Bennett was the third child born to Thomas Jefferson and Mary Bright Bennett. His father was a homestead farmer and evangelist who overcame physical challenges in his near blindness. His mother was an industrious and cultured caregiver who taught Bennett the importance of religion and education. His grandfather, George Washington Bennett, was a homestead farmer and horse trader with strong religious values. The importance of education to the family was seen when Henry, at age five, was moved to Arkadelphia, Arkansas, where the newly-established Ouachita College was located. The family built a boarding house where the college faculty boarded in exchange for tutoring the three Bennett children. With the tutoring and college preparatory classes, Bennett was able to graduate with a bachelor of arts degree in just two years of formal college classes.

During this period of education Bennett found time to assist with the family boarding house needs, work at local part-time jobs and secured a job as the first rural mail carrier in the state. He also traveled in the summers selling books across Kansas and the Indian Territory. His childhood friend and college forensics competitor was William Holloway, future governor of Oklahoma. They became lifelong friends.

After graduation, Bennett spent a brief time in Texarkana at a private business school that eventually went broke. Oklahoma had just obtained statehood and Bennett went back to selling books in the new state. In the small community of Boswell, Bennett was offered the job of school superintendent and teacher. The new state was unable to attract many teachers with college degrees and Bennett took the opportunity to rise in his profession, eventually becoming superintendent of schools for the Hugo school district. He invited his friend William Holloway to join his faculty. He married a teacher, and fellow Arkansan, Vera Connell in 1913. They started a family with the birth of their first two children. Bennett took the opportunity of teaching summer courses at the southeast Oklahoma college in Durant. His support of the school, interest in higher education and growing respect among local educators enabled him to become president of the two-year school in 1919.

For the next nine years, Bennett moved the two-year school to a nationally-recognized, four-year college. His "town and gown" philosophy allowed the school to grow with the community. He was an avid salesman for any student who wished to receive a college education in Durant. He provided boarding and financial assistance to many students from poor families. As college enrollment increased, new facilities and programs were created. The offering of summer and evening classes, short-term studies and extension programs earned Bennett national recognition for his innovative programs.

During this time in Durant, Bennett's friend William Holloway received his law degree and entered state politics with successes in local and state elections. He rose to the position of lieutenant governor and gained the respect of both opposing political parties for his fairness and work ethic. When the position of president for Oklahoma A & M College became open, Bennett was in a good position for the job because of his reputation and Holloway's influence.₇

Bennett's Arrival

In the summer of 1928 Bennett was recommended as one of several candidates for Oklahoma A & M College president in Stillwater, Oklahoma. There were the suspicions of Bennett being just another short-term, political appointee. Investigations by the Former Students Association reassured them of a conscientious and committed educator. He had amassed strong personal and public support for his progressive reforms at the Durant college. Within seven years at Oklahoma A & M, Bennett would change the political control of the college to a state higher education board and provide faculty with the security of tenured positions. Upon assuming leadership, he faced immense challenges that only strengthened confidence in his abilities and leadership. Bennett came prepared to lead with an amazing "twenty-five year plan" for the campus. This was immediately delayed due to the crisis of the Great Depression of 1929 that affected not only the country, but specifically the state and community. He used his influence and personal skills to keep the college functioning and even assisting the local communities. Much has and can be written of Bennett's accomplishments in his twenty-three years as the school's leader. In this work, it is necessary to focus on the international achievements Bennett personally led and those in which he involved Oklahoma Agricultural and Mechanical College.[8]

Henry Bennett had much international education experience before his involvement with President Truman's Point Four program of 1949. In 1931, just three years after his arrival in Stillwater, he traveled on a world tour for the twelfth district Rotary Club International. Having studied the beginnings of western universities in Italy, France and England, he was able to visit them. His exposure to the international educational, political and agricultural activities would lay the groundwork for his many accomplishments in the years ahead. In his December 14, 1931, Founders' Day speech, Bennett predicted that he would eventually "establish an international institute at the college to assist underdeveloped countries of the world to increase food production." This prophecy would find fulfillment within two decades.[9]

The experiences of World War II influenced Bennett's leadership at the college and broadened his worldview. The growing respect for Bennett on a national level was evidenced by his selection through the United States Agricultural Department to be a representative at the United Nation's first meeting of the International Food and Agricultural Organization in November 1945, in Quebec. He met with the other international representatives in dealing with the destruction and recovery of Europe following the war. He reported on the conference to his local newspaper and summarized that "technical assistance from some of the highly-developed countries will be sent to these undeveloped countries." Four years later the federal government would again call on Bennett's services to go on an eight-week assignment in Germany's Trizonia- the western divide controlled by the U.S., Great Britain and France. His task was to "assemble a survey suggesting development and progressive measures that would stabilize agricultural production." He reported his recommendations and final report to United States High Commissioner John J. McCloy. Many of his implemented recommendations were followed by dramatic improvements in that area's agricultural production. In completing this assignment, Bennett traveled over 25,000 miles.[10]

The Stillwater campus continued its attraction to international students seeking a college education. The registrar announced in 1948 that the institution now had enrolled men and women from twenty-eight different foreign countries. Bennett established the Office of International Programs two years later to directly assist the growing international enrollment.[11]

In 1950 Bennett was invited by Ethiopian Emperor, Haile Selassie, "to visit the North African country of Absysinia as advisor to Ethiopian educators and agriculturalists on the organization of an agricultural training center along the lines of land-grant colleges."[12] On his return trip to the United States, Bennett stopped in Washington, D. C. to visit with his friend Oklahoma Senator Robert Kerr, who realized the significance of Bennett's insights and scheduled a meeting with President Harry Truman. They shared their mutual beliefs of the need for educational aid to these underdeveloped, war-torn countries. Following the meeting, President Truman requested Kerr "to ask Bennett to write me a report of his trip to Ethiopia. I was very much impressed in what he had to say… and I would like to have a record of his conversation so I can give it more study." As a result of the trip, the Emperor accepted Bennett's recommendation to establish an agricultural college in Ethiopia with Bennett's leadership and an offer of help from the Oklahoma A & M faculty and staff.[13]

President Truman's surprising reelection in 1948 was followed by his equally surprising inclusion in his 1949 Inaugural Address of a fourth point outlining the administration's foreign policy following World War II. The State Department was caught off guard by the addition in the speech. It was a third-level State Department public relations employee, Benjamin Hardy, who surreptitiously met with the president's staff to develop the fourth point. The fourth point was a call for a national commitment to share technical assistance with the underdeveloped countries of the world. With a contentious Congress, Truman was able to get the program passed after yearlong efforts. He added another surprise by appointing a non-State Department, unlikely administrator, Henry Bennett of Oklahoma A & M College, in November 1950, to direct the Point Four program (later to become the United States Agency for International Development- USAID). Bennett agreed to the position subject to the approval of the college's board of regents. Following their approval and Bennett's agreement not to receive a salary from the state, Bennett began the process of defining the program, securing an organizational staff and authorizing adequate funding. With the addition of Ben Hardy and friends from other national departments, Bennett began to demonstrate his hands-on leadership with visits to determine needs and establish relationships with national leaders who would work cooperatively in program projects.[14]

The first project to receive Bennett's attention was in Ethiopia. His established friendship with Emperor Haile Selassie would lead to formalization of earlier plans in creating an agricultural education program in the country. Bennett asked Oklahoma A & M staff to visit Ethiopia and prepare for the program's implementation. Bennett and his wife, Vera, traveled with his staff on an extended visit to Central and South America in February and March 1951. By July 1951 Bennett was directing 139 projects in 34 countries with 397 Point Four technicians. In late 1951, Bennett, Vera and the staff left for a world tour to observe and evaluate the programs underway and assist in finalizing future programs. Their plans were to go to Rome, Italy; Athens, Greece; Cairo, Egypt; Amman, Jordan; Beirut, Lebanon; Damascus, Syria; Baghdad, Iraq; Teheran, Iran; Karachi, Pakistan; Dehli, Bombay, Colombo, Madras and Calcutta, India; Ceylon; Bangkok, Thailand; Hong Kong; and Tokyo, Japan. By mid-December the team, already days behind schedule, left Baghdad in perilous weather to fly northeast to Teheran to finalize program commitments with a contentious Iranian government. The plane made several attempts to land in a blinding snowstorm at the dangerous Mehrabad airport. The awaiting Point Four leaders and state department representatives assumed the plane had returned back to Baghdad in light of the storm. Early the next morning discovery of the plane wreckage was found two and a half miles north of the airport in the Elburz mountain range. All on board had died on impact. The bodies of Henry and Vera Bennett were found thrown clear of the wreckage still strapped in their seats with an open family Bible between them. The loss of Henry Bennett was felt not only by the Bennett family, but across the nation and the world. President Truman and world leaders mourned the loss of an important program director and a personal friend.[15]

In 1952, three hundred delegates from thirty-five countries met in Washington, D. C. for a conference sponsored by the International Economic and Social Development Agency. In honor of Henry Bennett they established and pledged funds to the Bennett Memorial Scholarship Fund that would allow over one thousand foreign students from underdeveloped countries to study agriculture and engineering in the United States without personal cost.[16]

Although Oklahoma A & M College had lost a legendary figurehead, the school continued under excellent leadership. A word of wisdom from an elderly minister was, "A sign of a great leader is not what things are done when the leader is present, but what continues after the leader is gone." A vibrant new president who continued the Bennett legacy was Oliver Willham. The important program that Bennett established in 1950, the Office of International Programs under William S. Abbott, would continue the international outreach effort for another forty years.[17]

Henry Garland Bennett and Ethiopian Emperor Haile Selaissie, Addas Ababa, Ethiopia, 1950.

President Harry S. Truman poses with members of his International Advisory Board. Fifth from the left is Henry G. Bennett.

Dr. Bennett with South American agriculturalist examining the fields.

Last known photo of Dr. and Mrs. Bennett with A.Cyril Crilly and James Hardy, Jerusalem, December 21, 1951.

Plane Wreckage in Iran Marks Spot where Dr. Bennett and wife died.

Bennett plane crash site marker in northern Iran, 1952. It reads in English and Farsi: "Dr. Henry Garland Bennett, Oklahoma Educator and Scholar, Director of Point Four, died here in an airplane accident December 22, 1951 at the age of 65 with his wife and four American associates."

Bennett Family and Ethiopian Emperor Haile Selassie, June 18, 1954, Oklahoma A&M College, Stillwater, Oklahoma.

Office of International Programs (1951-1990)

Need and Creation

As Bennett saw the future of Oklahoma A & M's international involvement growing, he realized the need for a strong program on campus to coordinate current and future international activities. In 1950, before Bennett's appointment as the Point Four director, he established the Office of International Programs (OIP). This office "provided support, stability, and continuity to Oklahoma State's international projects..."[18] One man stayed with the OIP from its inception—William S. Abbott. He was a graduate of the class of 1947 whose studies were interrupted by his military service as an Army anti-aircraft artillery officer in the southwest Pacific theater in World War II. After returning to college to complete his bachelor's degree, he shared a meaningful personal experience with Henry Bennett, who had just returned from first Point Four trip to Ethiopia. In a Sunday School class taught by Bennett, Abbott and Bennett shared thoughts about poverty in the Third World. Having accepted an administrative position on campus, Abbott became a strong supporter of the 185 Oklahoma A & M College faculty and staff families working in Ethiopia. This led to his appointment as the first director of the OIP. It was said that Abbott "had Bennett's heart of helping international students." Abbott would continue uninterrupted leadership for the OIP until his retirement in the fall of 1991.[19]

Bennett knew this position needed to have strong authority and autonomy to survive the usual academic fights for power and funds. OIP was autonomous with independent funding and answerable only to the college president. As the number of international students arrived at Stillwater for undergraduate and graduate classes and the number of international projects sponsored by the college increased, the activities of the OIP also grew. Funding was provided through foundation grants, contractual education agreements and private funds. The need for special services for international students became necessary. Temporary loans were provided as needed to international students awaiting currency exchanges and transfers. Similarly, faculty and staff needed preparation and assistance for foreign travel and living experiences. The OIP worked with foundations for project funding and cooperated with the newly-established academic schools of study when Oklahoma A & M College's name was changed to Oklahoma State University in 1957. These schools, especially agriculture, home economics, business and engineering, were becoming aware of opportunities to establish their own international projects following the model of the Ethiopian experiences. It was reported that "the more Oklahoma A & M College exported its expertise to Third World countries by sending members of its faculty abroad, the more international students came to the Stillwater campus for a college education." From 1957 through 1980, the OSU Department of Agricultural Education provided courses in instructional procedures, adult education and group dynamics for 412 students from 37 developing countries. "Nearly half of the students received a degree with many eventually earning a master's degree."[20]

One of the reasons for the university's continued, effective international education efforts was the OIP and its freedom of operation. Even after Bennett's tragic death, Oklahoma A & M President Willham continued Bennett's organizational approach to international involvement. Enhancing the OIP's activities was the 1978 addition of Conrad Evans as associate director. Evans and his family had served for thirteen years in Ethiopia in the continued OSU education projects. His first-hand international experience and interest in continuing the training of international students added another big heart to the growing organization.[21] The OIP expanded its services with additional programs such as the English Language Institute. Kay W. Keys served as its director from its addition in the summer of 1970.

It was stated that through the years the OIP "provided as many services for the OSU campus as the State Department of the federal government." The organization would, over time, develop the responsibilities for the following services:

- Acting as an official point of access and contact with government and other agencies regarding international contracts
- Disseminating information about grant and contract possibilities involving foreign governments, foundations and international organizations
- Assisting with the development of proposals for contracts

between OSU and international organizations, foreign governments and other organizations
- Serving as a point of contact for international visitors
- Assisting in the recruitment of international students and offering extended services to the sponsored, contract and special international students
- Administering special programs and international projects
- Assisting with the maintenance of contact with international OSU alumni
- Administering the Study Abroad Programs
- Tracking OSU international involvement[22]

Although the OIP would evolve as an organization, academic struggles and changes in the campus leadership would eventually lead to a deterioration of its effectiveness. As contracts became more competitive with other universities and international events affected the recruitment efforts, the funding of the OIP became a burden to the university. After forty years of valued leadership, its independent status was weakened by the direct activities of the schools within the university and incorporation with other university programs. Following a careful analysis of the program needs, leadership changes and financial cost ineffectiveness, it was necessary to bring the OIP under the umbrella of the University Extension, International and Economic Development department in 1997.

International Impact

Throughout the first century of the university's unique history, 1890 to 1990, many international events influenced the international activities on and off campus. These international events caused disruptions as well as opportunities for the school in the international programs. The experiences of American involvement opened the eyes of many World War I American soldiers and families to a world map that was before largely ignored. The first-hand encounters of then Oklahoma A & M's student soldiers in international countries and cultures created the opportunity for building relationships that would directly affect the university with an influx of international students desirous of an education. For international students, the ravages of the war on their countries illuminated the need for educated leaders to return to rebuild the cities and reclaim the needed food production of the land. However, the war also drew the United States into an isolationist national foreign policy. The failure of international programs such as the League of Nations was due to the lack of support by the United States.

Along with the isolationist mentality came domestic crises that challenged the ability of the country and Oklahoma schools to focus on any international needs. The Great Depression of 1929 along with the Dust Bowl of the 1930s, caused many educational institutions to be preoccupied with survival. Oklahoma A & M, under Bennett's early leadership, sought to tighten its economic belt to keep its operation going while trying to assist Payne County and the state in their economic and agricultural needs. The effect of the Great Depression was so strongly felt in the United States that it was easy to forget the global impact of such a crisis. Many internationally-related businesses and foundations felt the economic losses and were unable to provide the humanitarian and business investments that were so desperately needed around the world.

As discontent increased within war-torn and underdeveloped countries, the opportunity arose for new political dictatorships and philosophies. In Russia, communism claimed a stronghold. In Germany and Italy, national socialism began its domination. Under the guise of benefiting the people, these political parties sought to use human and natural resources for their own power and control. The rise of strong dictators and cruel human atrocities did little to move the western countries from isolationist foreign policies. The resulting growth of powerful dictators and unopposed political parties laid the groundwork for another world war.

During this time, the influx of immigrants to the United States provided the opportunity for an increase of international students in the U. S. colleges and universities. Many of the wealthier foreign families had the ability to move to the security of their new country. They wanted the best education for their children and many wanted additional education for their professions. Schools such as Oklahoma A & M would provide that opportunity. The outbreak of war in Europe caught the attention of the American public, but there was a lingering desire to remain uninvolved. With the attack on Pearl Harbor December 7, 1941, the United States became actively involved in World War II. A new generation of Americans provided military support necessary around the world. Oklahoma A & M was one of many schools who prepared young men and women to face the demands of military action. One of these groups trained was the Women Accepted for Volunteer Emergency Services (WAVES).[23] Oklahoma A & M saw its students enlist in the war cause, including the sons of Henry Bennett.

As students returned to campus after the war, they brought with them new relationships and visions of the human devastation of war. They also brought back a new understanding for international students on campus with whom they could share world experiences they now had in common. OSU also provided educational opportunities to prepare returning veterans for new professions, especially with the creation of the G. I. Bill.

On a national level, new leadership under President Harry Truman led the United States to meet humanitarian needs of countries devastated by the war. The need for an end of isolationism was evident if another world war was to be prevented. The creation of the United Nations and the support of the United States would be an important factor for world peace. Another consideration in foreign policy was the threat of an expansion of communism. Oklahoma A & M's direct involvement in these new foreign policy efforts would be realized in the selection by President Truman of Henry Bennett to lead the new Point Four program to provide cooperative technical assistance to the underdeveloped countries of the world. Bennett's past international trips to Germany and Ethiopia would provide the background for the program's success. The Point Four program was also an extension of the purpose of a land-grant college on an international level. As the program intended to meet the threat of communist propaganda, it also provided the opportunity for Americans to become personally involved in making a difference internationally. Oklahoma A & M began its first of many international projects in Ethiopia. This saw the recruitment of many Ethiopians to be trained at the Stillwater campus. The diplomatic war against communism was won in those countries where the Point Four program was strongest- Ethiopia, India and Iran.[24]

Later international conflicts would affect the number of international students that would come to Stillwater. The Korean War and the later Vietnam War would decrease the number of international students from those affected countries. As the United States sought to rebuild war-torn countries the number of international students increased. Later the Iranian crisis would create a decrease in the students from Iran. These international crises also affected the local community of Stillwater in its relations with some international students. There were more incidents of open hostility toward some of these international students, even in instances of mistaking the student's country of origin. It was reported that these international students on campus "all too frequently experienced what other minority groups experienced- misunderstanding, discrimination in housing and stores, racism, and few friendships with Americans."[25] Awareness of these negative experiences led the school to develop organizations with the intent of helping the campus community to be more inclusive and supportive of the international students in the day-to-day activities at the university.

In these times of international crises, the university adapted to meet the continuing need of training and education for international students. The university also provided the necessary education for American students to personally assist in international programs. Beyond the university's ongoing international programs, such as study abroad, new national programs were established to give OSU students additional opportunities for international service. In 1962, the Peace Corps was established and many OSU students responded with sacrificial commitment to improve the world- one community at a time.[26] Other such programs would be created under the university administrations to encourage international participation of American students to serve abroad.

Part Two:
Leading and Learning

"Several important factors influenced OSU's emphasis in international education; the most important was the leadership provided by three presidents [Bennett, Willham and Kamm] who served during this quarter-century."
(*The Great Adventure*, Jerry Leon Gill, 1978, page 122)

"Those who share their knowledge gain insight and new experience."
(Henry Garland Bennett, Point Four Director, 1951)

"The people we train represent the leaders of their nations. The opportunity to learn from them, and them from us, gives the title of 'university' its ultimate meaning by becoming universal."
(William S. Abbott, Director, OSU Office of International Programs from 1951-1991) (*International Programs, Centennial Histories Series*, Jerry L. Gill, 1991)

"This was the great challenge, to impart our technology to people in such a way that they could do it themselves... And then to learn, if possible, from the good things they have been doing and proceed from there rather than assuming that we have all the answers beforehand."
(Conrad Evans, Dedication Proceedings, School of International Studies, April 1, 1999)

Original International Programs Purposes

After sixty years of university-wide international education, OSU has created a great legacy of experience and has enjoyed continued supportive leadership. From these years of unique experiences, OSU has been fortunate to learn some valuable and practical lessons in the field of international studies. From the international education pioneer days of President Henry Bennett to the modern days of President Lawrence Boger, lessons were learned from mutual international exchanges. From President Boger until the present, new lessons were learned from the formation of the School of International Studies. It is important for the university to be aware of and focus on evaluating its past lessons to benefit its present international education experiences.

Bennett to Boger Lessons

Henry Bennett's experiences were unique in his leadership of the Point Four program. He learned the value of *organization* internationally, nationally and even on a university campus level. The Point Four program required a cooperative effort to involve and benefit the countries to be assisted. There were carefully drafted international agreements that required organized efforts of accountability and patience. To secure continued national support, there was a need for an organization to provide effective public relations to the American citizens and to the Congress. Bennett was also aware that for the continued support of the programs presented to the Oklahoma A & M campus, there was a need for structural and effective organization. Bennett created the Office of International Programs to coordinate the campus participation. Bennett also wisely allowed Oklahoma A & M Vice President Oliver Wilham to oversee campus international education efforts.[1] With Bennett's sudden death in December 1951, the Oklahoma A & M campus would continue to lead in the international assistance programs because of the organization that had been in place.

Another important lesson learned from Bennett's leadership was an attitude of *mutual learning* in international experiences. In many of the public relations speeches that Bennett gave to American audiences, he often reminded the audience of how the United States had borrowed much from other civilizations. In an article that he wrote, which was published two months after his death, he expressed the extent of our borrowing. He stated that Americans borrowed people from around the world. We borrowed the "principles that guide our political and moral conduct." We borrowed "liberally from many cultures. The Phoenicians gave us our alphabet. Our numbers are Arabic. Every line we speak or write owes something to Sanskrit, Greek, Latin, German or a Romance language." In the areas of agriculture, Bennett was quick to point out the many things we have borrowed:

> Europe gave us wheat, rye, oats and barley. Our winter wheat came to us from Turkey—by way of Russia. The Orient gave us rice.

> From the Middle East we obtained asparagus, beets, broccoli, cabbage, cauliflower, celery, endive, kale, lettuce, parsley, parsnips and rhubarb; from South Asia and the Far East black-eyed peas, cucumbers, eggplant, mustards, soybeans and sugarcane; from Africa sorghums, watermelons and coffee.

> Our multi-billion-dollar dairy and beef industries are founded on breeding stock imported from Great Britain, Western Europe and India; for milk, the Guernsey and Jersey of the Channel Isles; the Holstein of the Low Countries; the Ayrshire of Scotland; for beef, the Shorthorn and the Hereford of England, the Aberdeen-Angus of Scotland; the Zebu and Brahma of India.[2]

Bennett also reminded us that the American pastures were covered with the clovers of Europe and the alfalfa of Persia. From the Indians of North America, we received corn or maize, white and sweet potatoes, squashes, pumpkins, green and yellow snap beans, peas, kidney and lima beans, peppers and tomatoes. He also indicated that "our present and future welfare depends on our foreign sources of supply." Among these were tin and rubber from Malaysia, wool from Australia, manganese from India, copper from Chile, hemp from the Philippines, coffee from Brazil, tea from Ceylon, bananas from Central America, sugar from Cuba and spices and medicinal products from many corners of the globe.[3]

Bennett reminded us that we all owe mutual debts of borrowing.

If Point Four was a program mostly of education, it was a two-way street. Conrad Evans, an OSU faculty member who served with Point Four many years in Ethiopia, related one experience that illustrates how we can learn from the agricultural practices of other countries. Evans indicated that when they left for Ethiopia, they went with an attitude of invincibility and had all of the answers to the Ethiopian needs. They brought with them hybrid corn for production in Ethiopia. With great pride they planted the corn in their field and watched the plants grow and mature ready for harvest only to be unavailable because of the continued heavy rains. The hybrid corn was bred for a certain number of days that was not suitable to the climate of Ethiopia. Evans concluded:

> There was a valuable lesson to be learned there. Thankfully we were flexible, adaptable, astute observers. It dawned on us that these people had been raising corn for hundreds of years, and they are still doing it. They must have been doing something right. So as Dr. [Morris] Baker said, it behooves us to find out what they have been doing. And then to learn, if possible, from the good things that they have been doing and proceed from there rather than assuming we have all of the answers beforehand. Consequently, we came back a much wiser group than when we left. And this spirit of finding out where we were, who the people we were working with were, created a friendship and environment that still is ongoing today.[4]

The requirement of *university-wide support* was another important lesson learned from the early years. With Bennett as president, it was easier to achieve this requirement on the Oklahoma A & M campus. He had the respect and credibility of international experiences from his years of national service after World War II. After Bennett's death and the change of Oklahoma A & M to Oklahoma State University, it was more difficult to keep university-wide support. The creation of the various colleges in the university increased the difficulty of communication and awareness of international opportunities and activities for the entire campus. The competition from other educational institutions as well as the increasing number of non-governmental organizations made access to funding more difficult. Some of the university's colleges had more natural ties to international education experiences than others. Over time, this would create indifference for international activities in some of the colleges. It became the role of the college dean or an aggressive faculty member to pursue access to funding for the competitive international projects. The waning power and aggressive leadership of the Office of International Programs added to the loss of university-wide support.

Boger to Hargis Lessons

Lawrence Boger observed a university with decreasing growth in numbers and facilities. He also saw a university that had lost its *unified support and involvement* in international outreach and education. With the absence of effective international program leadership and only limited administrative involvement, the university's colleges kept the international activities continuing. This decentralization created pockets of traditional international activities only within several of the many colleges on campus. Presidential leadership on campus was distracted by budget challenges, faculty and staff turnover and domestic student recruitment. Growing competition for funding international programs with other universities and non-government organizations created additional difficulties. In the arrival of Presidents James Halligan and Burns Hargis, there was a rediscovery of Henry Bennett and his important role in the university's unique identity. The School of International Studies was allowed to give the history and significance of Henry Bennett a proper place on campus.

International events would create opportunities for rediscovery of the OSU commitment to international education. With the elimination of the Berlin Wall and the fall of the Soviet Union, openings were created for new and needed international outreach programs similar in nature to the Point Four efforts after World War II. Boger, retired, and a group of visionary faculty members were quick to take advantage of this opportunity with securing funds and traveling to those countries in eastern Europe hungry for education in free enterprise, agriculture and economic development.[5] They also saw the need to rediscover a centralized program on campus to coordinate international education and outreach. Through their persistent pursuits over a number of years, they found success in the establishment of the School of International Studies. During more than a decade of existence, the SIS had found increasing support in

James Halligan and a growing awareness of the university's legacy and opportunities. As noted earlier, this same philosophy has been so competently followed by current President Burns Hargis.

Academic Priorities

One of the ongoing frustrations in identifying the international programs at OSU is the confusion of program titles. In publications and signage there is confusion between the School of International Studies and the International Education and Outreach. The unique aspect of the academically-based School of International Studies best describes the campus role. The title International Education and Outreach comparatively is a limiting concept with no recognition of the strong academic discipline involving and equal to the other schools of study on campus. The graduate program was established with a challenging academic curriculum on par with other nationally-recognized international study programs. If the program is to be recognized on campus as a legitimate "school" of studies, it needs to be directed by an equally recognized "dean" as it was originally. The present School of International Studies has within its organization an active department of International Education and Outreach which also adds to the confusion.

Other colleges and universities may have international studies programs that are little more than short-term study abroad opportunities. But most are not academically based and few offer a master's degree level of true international studies. The OSU School of International Studies needs to continue to clarify its significant role on campus and in public relations both nationally and internationally.

Competition

New challenges faced the university with the creation of the United States Agency for International Development (USAID). The heir of the Point Four program found success or failure according to the national administration leadership changes. The Eisenhower administration changed the tactics of the Point Four program result-ing in the reputation of the "ugly American" foreign policy. The Kennedy administration seemed to rediscover some of the Point

Four concepts with the creation of USAID and the Peace Corps. Unpopular foreign entanglements in Vietnam in the 1960-1970s led to decreases in USAID budget and programs. The Nixon administration began a slow process of improving USAID budget, but more of a continuation of the Eisenhower foreign policies. The Carter administration was embroiled in economic crisis and a foreign crisis in Iran. The Reagan/Bush administrations led in an era of not only decreased funds for USAID, but opened the funds to more favored private corporations instead of the traditional higher education involvement. The Clinton administration increased the funding for USAID but began a program of "outsourcing" programs to international leadership. The following Bush administration was sidetracked in the use of funds because of involvement in international wars in Iraq and Afghanistan. The Obama administration rediscovered the benefit of a more involved and better funded USAID.

The use of the USAID funding created a challenge for universities. With decreasing funds available, competition among a growing number of schools and the non-government organizations, OSU was challenged to discover new sources of revenue for the international programs. Private corporations and private donations were aggressively sought by the well-connected leadership in the schools of business and agriculture. OSU would have an edge in the competitive field with the establishment of the SIS. This program gave academic credibility and international experience from its historical legacy. The assistance of the SIS Ambassadors organization opened new doors for operating funds, scholarships and international program assistance.

Recent International Impacts

Since the School of International Studies' creation in 1999, there have been international events that have had great impact on the international studies at OSU. The fateful terrorist attack on the World Trade Center of September 11, 2001, had a mixed impact on campus. There was the immediate anger and intimidation of any international student of Arab descent or appearance. Even so, the number of international students increased to record numbers in the following two years.[6] It was suggested that many international students from the east and west coast schools transferred to more secure area of mid-America. The SIS experienced an increase of enrollment of domestic students desiring a need for more understanding of international affairs.

The devastation of the second Iraq war also created an opportunity for OSU to help in the rebuilding of Iraq's education program. In 2005 OSU's School of International Studies program assisted in training at the Al-Nahrain and Salahaddin Universities.[7]

Various economic challenges affected the OSU international programs. One primary example was the collapse of the Mexican currency in 1994-1995. President Clinton assisted the bailout of the Mexican economy with domestically unpopular loans to stabilize the Mexican currency. Although Mexico recovered and paid back the loans, the economic crisis in Mexico dramatically affected the number of student exchanges with Mexico and OSU. An expanding exchange program with Mexico and OSU was set back until their economy stabilized. In 1997 Japan suffered from an economic meltdown. The resulting affect on the Japanese economy limited the growing number of exchange students with OSU. OSU programs in Japan were also affected with the economic crisis. Japanese families were unable to continue sending their students to the OSU-sponsored education programs underway in Japan at the time. This resulted in the discontinuation of OSU education efforts in Japan at that time. When the United States experienced drops in the value of the dollar, foreign investment in the U. S. increased and the number of international students able to afford an American education increased affecting OSU in a positive way. With the global economic crisis of 2000, international educational programs were affected in several ways. The availability of endowed scholarship funds decreased. Funding for international programs also decreased and became more competitive. The economic crisis directly affected OSU in operational budget cuts and even more careful scrutiny of expenditures. The search for new revenue sources for the SIS programs was made more difficult with potential donors being more cautious of gifts for education.

Another impact in the international community on education programs was the rapid rise of dangerous health epidemics. These epidemics caused travel restrictions and precautionary measures that made international more difficult. In 2003 the Severe Acute Respiratory Syndrome (SARS) scare moved quickly from China to thirty-seven other countries. This affected routine travel and student exchange programs. In 2009 the rapid increase in what was called the swine flu (H1N1) also affected concern for international travel and student exchange programs. At OSU the impact was quite apparent. Jose Sagarnaga, the Mexico-OSU Liaison Manager, had spent much time and effort to coordinate the recurring summer program for fifty students from Mexico to come to OSU for several weeks of study. The program was cancelled just before the planned trip, as was all other faculty, staff and student travel to Mexico that summer, because of fears regarding the growing swine flu epidemic.[8] International trips and crossing of borders were greatly complicated by the cautions regarding the epidemic. The impact was certainly felt on other international educational institutions as many such programs were cancelled.

Transition Period (1990-1999)

A ten-year transition period, from 1990-1999, would witness organizational restructuring, leadership definition, financial challenges and an expansion of an academic discipline in international studies. The oversight of all university international programs was very decentralized. The individual schools were directing their own international activities and providing needed services for their international students. Individual faculty members, through their own interest sand initiatives, would apply for grants for specific short-term projects. Several factors came together during this period to prepare the way for the creation of the School of International Studies including the economy and university budget; the Center for International Trade and Development; a tireless pursuit for centralization of the international programs; a new university president, James Halligan; and a consolidation of traditional programs that were no longer cost-effective.

First, national and state economies were deeply affected by the loss of oil and energy revenue. The state and university relied heavily upon the income from oil production and increasing prices. In the late 1980s the oil pricing began to drop rapidly. Revenue in the state began to drop correspondingly. State allocations for higher education suffered along with other programs. The impact at OSU was dramatic. At one point the deans of the schools were asked to cut their annual budget by as much as 14 percent.[9] As state income decreased on a local basis, the higher education enrollment began to drop. The enrollment at OSU dropped for thirteen consecutive years from the mid-1980s and throughout the early 1990s.[10] International programs were limited and mostly initiated by individual faculty members able to receive competitive grants and outside financial support.

Second, the establishment of the Center for International Trade Development (CITD) provided the physical space for a centralized international program. The concept for this far-reaching program was solely the idea and energy of Oklahoma Third District Congressman Wes Watkins. In March 1985, Watkins had helped an Oklahoma group export energy technology to Indonesia. The OSU Board of Regents formally endorsed the academic commitment for CITD "support for understanding and assisting the processes of international trade development."[11] After Wes Watkins successfully raised the necessary funds for the building construction, approved guidelines formed the CITD mission statement as follows:

- The primary focus of the Center is the development of international trade in Oklahoma as a vital component of continuing state economic development.
- Programs in support of international trade development will be enhanced or established for each of the missions of the land-grant university- teaching, research and extension.
- The Center will seek to develop faculty awareness of the international interdependence and its implications and to support and encourage related research, study, foreign experience and professional development.
- The Center will work to establish regional leadership in coordinating and stimulating academic programs in international trade development and in providing linkage with the national trade policy establishment, e.g. federal governments, trade policy research institutes and trade associations.
- Programs and activities of the Center will complement and support the objectives and operations of other federal, state and local public and private groups and agencies participating in the total network of Oklahoma international trade development assistance. Appropriate representation of these

groups will be involved early in the planning process to ensure cooperation and limit duplication of effort.[12]

A formal proposal, made by Congressman Wes Watkins to the United State Department of Agriculture Cooperative State Research Services, was approved in October 1986. Groundbreaking for the new facility was held on April 22, 1988. A $5 million matching grant from United States Department of Agriculture (USDA) was met through state and private funds.[13] The impact of providing the $5 million of matching funds from the state was felt on the campus with fewer funds being available for the university's colleges. This created some resentment on campus with having to delay planned projects and activities. The facility was opened in 1990 and later named the Wes Watkins Center for International Trade Development in 1998. The facility had to comply with federal guidelines for use. The 80,000 square foot facility included an auditorium, a multipurpose exhibit hall, catering kitchen, dining areas, presentation rooms and offices. Initially, the CITD began with a flurry of programs and international trade possibilities. A full-time director was secured and the facility began to increase in use.[14] But the economic downturn of the 1990s hit the program hard. Limited state funds, poor CITD administrative leadership and waning university support left the facility unable to achieve its self-supporting status by 1993. The facility was only in limited use and serious state interest in international trade development had shifted to internal needs. The CITD, along with the OIP, was also incorporated into the University Extension, International and Economic Development (UEIED) in July 1997.[15]
The third factor, was the tireless pursuit for centralization of the international programs by a group of dedicated and committed faculty and administration. On January 3, 1990, OSU President John R. Campbell gave a report that reviewed the university's international programs. The report drew heavily upon an earlier 1981 International Studies and Programs Task Force Report under the leadership of President Lawrence Boger. President Campbell's report emphasized three areas of concerns: to strengthen the university's commitment to international involvement; maintain a strong academic standard; and involve the entire university in its activities.[16] These three areas would be critical in forming the foundation

for the School of International Studies. While the OIP maintained an important but diminished role in meeting international student needs and public relations, it would be ten years before a structural organization would be created to return to the original purposes of OSU's international assistance. On May 20, 1992, an International Programs Advisory Council Report endorsed the 1990 report and encouraged its implementation.[17] After a decade of frustrating and patient persistence, a committee of representatives from the academic schools of study and administration, presented their recommendations that would find a welcome ear from new university leadership. Among the key leaders in this long-term project were Lawrence Boger, Robert Sandmeyer, David Henneberry, James Osborn, Stephen Miller and James Hromas. These men had been meeting as early as the late 1980s in an informal committee to explore means for an international agriculture-business major and outreach program. With the fall of the Soviet Union, they secured USAID funds to travel to the new Eastern Europe countries to teach free enterprise.[18] They had no personal agenda other than increasing international awareness from an academic perspective.

Lawrence Boger was the fourteenth president of Oklahoma State University, serving from 1977-1988. He brought educational experiences from Purdue University and Michigan State University in leading the College of Agriculture and Natural Resources and in university administration. During his time as OSU president the enrollment for international students reached a peak in 1981. He implemented many international initiatives, including a branch office in Japan and an agricultural research project in Morocco. In 1981, he established a committee to report on the growing international programs on campus. He was later honored to be the first recipient of the Henry G. Bennett Distinguished Fellow Award.[19] It was stated, "the vision which formed the foundation for the School of International Studies reflects Dr. Boger's dedication to extending the legacy of international studies at Oklahoma State University."[20]

Robert Sandmeyer received an OSU education. After receiving his Ph. D., he was hired in 1962 as a visiting assistant professor. He continued his service to OSU for over forty years, most significantly as the dean of the College of Business Administration for seventeen years. He aggressively promoted economic development in Oklahoma. His growing interest in international outreach began immediately upon his retirement from OSU by serving in Al Ain, United Arab Emirates (UAE) as adviser to the Minister of Higher Education and Scientific Research and the dean and a faculty member of the College of Business and Economics at UAE University for one year. He served on various OSU international advisory committees and authored the concept paper for the OSU School of International Studies for its establishment in 1999. He is credited with insisting on the strong academic basis of the SIS. In 2001, he served as dean of the College of Business Sciences at UAE's Zayed University. In 2004, he served as a consultant for a United States Agency for International Development project in Amman, Jordan. He was also honored as an OSU Henry G. Bennett Distinguished Fellow Award recipient.[21]

David Henneberry served actively on the OSU international advisory committees and has served OSU in the College of Agricultural Sciences and Natural Resources for twenty-five years in the area of international agricultural trade and as assistant dean. In 1999 he served as director of the International Agricultural Programs. He continues to be a strong proponent of international study and program experiences for those in the College of Agricultural Sciences and Natural Resources. He served on the Executive Committee of the School of International Studies.[22]

James Osborn has served in the OSU College of Agriculture since 1979. He served as faculty and eventually as assistant dean of the College of Agriculture until his retirement in 1999. He began his international experiences in Honduras, Costa Rica, Mexico and Eastern Europe. He also served faithfully on OSU's international advisory committees. Others commented on how he never missed a meeting. Although very little is written about his contributions on the committees, his faithfulness, on-the-field experiences and effectiveness in enlisting faculty and staff support made major contributions to the establishment of the School of International Studies.[23]

Stephen Miller served as the director of the Graduate Programs for the SIS. He comes from an educational background at OSU, UCLA and Penn State University. He has served OSU the past thirty years as a professor of marketing and as director of the International Business Program in the OSU College of Business Administration. He has traveled and lectured extensively throughout many countries and serves as a member of the Governor's International Team to enhance the state's global competitiveness. He led in the application of telecommunication technologies for the campus's distance learning programs. He served on the OSU international advisory committees.[23]

James Hromas has actively served OSU for over forty years. He brought business experience with AMOCO and the NASA Space Center to his work at OSU. He has worked on projects, presented at conferences and traveled throughout many countries. Beginning in July 1997, he chaired the campus international advisory committee that developed the curriculum and recommended the structure which led to the establishment of the OSU School of International Studies. He has served as director of Business Extension in the Spears School of Business Administration and served as the director of International Education and Outreach program. He also chaired the OSU Outreach Council and the International Advisory Council. He is active in the Sister Cities International leadership, serving on its international board of directors and secretary of the executive committee. He has been described as "the driving force within OSU Outreach and a catalyst for change bringing OSU to regional, national and international recognitions through his outreach and international efforts."[25] He was the recipient of the 2008 Great Plains University Continuing Education Association (UCEA) John L. Christopher Outstanding Leadership Award and he has continued for ten years as the first director of the OSU School of International Studies. In 2009 he was honored with the Walton S. Bittner Service Citation, the highest award given by the UCEA. In 2013 he presented the Henry G. Bennett Distinguished Fellow Award.[26]

There were other significant contributors to the committee work. One of the key advisors and consultants was Richard W. Poole. He worked behind the scenes as a university administrator to make the international studies plans work. After distinguished military service, Poole began a 33 year career at OSU serving in all academic ranks from instructor, full professor, dean of the College of Business and as university vice president. The university Regents designated him as "Regents Distinguished Service Professor." In 1999 he was presented the Henry G. Bennett Distinguished Service Award. His knowledge of university policy and politics provided valuable assistance in the creation of the SIS.[27]

The final committee assignments emphasized the broad faculty and academic schools involvement and support. The Administrative Committee was composed of the deans of each of the seven participating colleges and Dean of the University Extension and International Education Development (UEIED). Committee members were Sam Curl, dean, Agricultural Sciences and Natural Resources; Smith Holt, dean, Arts and Sciences; Gary Trennpohl, dean, Business Administration; Ann Candler-Lotven, dean, Education; Karl Reid, dean, Engineering, Architecture and Technology; Wayne Powell, dean, Graduate College; Patricia Knaub, dean, Human Environmental Sciences, and; James Hromas, dean, UIEIED.[28]

The original development committee and later Executive Committee was composed of one faculty member from each of the participating colleges and the deans of the Graduate College and UEIED. Committee members were Jim Osborn, assistant dean, Agricultural Sciences and Natural Resources; Bruce Crauder, associate dean, Arts and Sciences; Gerald Lage, associate dean, Business Administration; Ed Harris, associate dean, Education; Bjong Yeigh, assistant professor, Engineering, Architecture and Technology; Donna Branson, Design, Housing and Merchandising Head, Human Environmental Sciences; Wayne Powell, dean, Graduate College, and; James Hromas, dean, UEIED, as chair.[29]

The fourth factor preparing the way for the establishment of the OSU School of International Studies was the arrival of OSU's sixteenth president James Halligan. He brought with him educational experiences from Iowa State University and New Mexico State University where he served as president. He came to OSU as president in 1994 and served in that capacity until 2003.[30] He arrived at a very difficult time in the university's history. The economic bust of the 1980s hit the campus hard and President Halligan led efforts to stop the thirteen consecutive years of declining enrollment. In a direct and forthright manner he required severe cuts within the colleges to maintain an operating budget. The realism of the university's situation required what he called a "grow or die" philosophy. He saw the increase of student credit hours as the key to increasing funding. When the International Agribusiness Committee presented its recommendations, President Halligan saw an opportunity to centralize the campus's international outreach and bring in new undergraduate and graduate students. The recommendations also provided the opportunity to incorporate struggling outreach programs into one area of control and supervision. The number of international students coming to OSU increased to record numbers in the years immediately following the 9/11 attacks in New York City in 2001. He was able to lead the university in generating funds for new campus facilities and encourage the campus in expanding research and economic development programs. In 2008 he successfully ran for state senator in Oklahoma where he currently serves.[31]

The fifth factor preparing the way for the establishment of the OSU School of International Studies was the consolidation of the waning university international outreach programs. The Office of International Programs, while still active, had lost its ability for financial self-support and had changed leadership. The Center for International Trade and Development had suffered from economic hardships and poor administration. These programs were no longer cost-effective in a very difficult economic period. The university needed to be mindful of the outreach traditions while efficient in the program operations. As proposed by Hromas, and supported by Provost Marvin Keener and James Halligan, the 1997 consolidation of these programs was changed into the University Extension, International and Economic Development program.[32] In 2004, under the Schmidly administration, the name was changed to the International Education and Outreach program and the budget was cut by 60 percent.[33]

In spite of the economic hard times and decentralization of international programs, there were many international activities underway during this transition period. The Office of International Programs reported that during this transition period, 1990-1999, there were sixty-two international projects completed in the following twenty-six countries: Belize, Botswana, Brazil, Bulgaria, Chile, China, Ecuador, Ethiopia, Former Soviet Union, Guatemala, Honduras, Hungary, India, Indonesia, Japan, Kazakhstan, Korea, Mexico, Morocco, Peru, Poland, South Africa, Tanzania, Thailand, Turkey and Venezuela. There were seven other projects listed as "Worldwide" in which OSU participated.[34]

With an increasing number of international students returning to OSU and an increasing interest by American students in international awareness, there was a need to centralize the efforts of the consolidated programs and expand a graduate program in international studies. The ongoing activities of international programs within the colleges and the desire to reach new students on a graduate level came together in the creation of the School of International Studies.

Creation of the School of International Studies (1999)

The growth of international involvement for the Oklahoma State University campus can be attributed largely to outstanding leadership. That leadership always originated from university presidents with a worldview and personal interest in international educational affairs. Among those were Henry Bennett, Oliver Willham, Robert Kamm, Lawrence Boger and James Halligan. The campus is fortunate to have such a president in that leadership role today, Burns Hargis. From the very early beginning of the university's history with international students, key leadership has also come from dedicated campus faculty and staff. That holds very true today and will be the secret of successful international ventures in the future.

The demise of the Office of International Programs, the continuation of campus international programs and activity, and the growth of international students attending OSU on an undergraduate and graduate level, caused a need for centralization of the scattered international programs on campus. There was also a strong desire for an international studies academic discipline. These dreams would find fulfillment in the School of International Studies, a path of a long two-year journey led by a team of dedicated faculty and staff.

Strategic Planning

On July 9, 1997, former OSU president Lawrence Boger sent a letter to then OSU president James Halligan outlining the results of the informal committee pursuing the goal "to raise the visibility of existing international activities and to consider the possible new ones for OSU," including the creation of a "School of International Studies."[35] These ideas, now coming from a more formal International Agribusiness Committee, were communicated to the Dean's Council with largely favorable response. A draft for the School of International Studies was created by Dr. Robert

Sandmeyer. This concept germinated at a lunch meeting with Sandmeyer and Hromas in February 1997. University Extension, International and Economic Development Dean James Hromas was asked to take the lead in involving the deans and faculty to "refine the concept and develop proposed programs" by the time of January 20, 1999, the 50th anniversary of the announcement of President Truman's Point Four program. The functions of teaching, research and extension were to be included with intercollegiate cooperation. President Halligan and the University Committee endorsed the concept and presented the proposal to the Board of Regents. On July 24, 1998, the Board of Regents approved the School of International Studies (SIS) with Dr. James Hromas as dean.[36]

Academic Priority

An overriding requirement for the new program was a strong academic base. While other nationally noted models were examined; such as John Hopkins, Georgetown, George Washington, Michigan State, Thunderbird, South Carolina and other universities;[37] meetings were held with the committee to discover classes appropriate for curriculum development. A graduate level program would require faculty involvement with no additional incentives. There would be academic positives and negatives to such a graduate program. The positives would be greater intercollegiate involvement and assurance of graduate-level classes being offered. The negatives would be increased class sizes, faculty assistance for personal international studies needs and non-undergraduate background of some international studies students within the schools. Four faculty members would deliver the four core courses and students could choose ongoing classes in over forty focus area courses.[38] It was important that the leadership of this program be recognized as a dean of the new school. This would allow continued communication with the Dean's Council and maintenance of the high academic standards of the other established schools of study.

Structural Plans

With the school's approval, a dean appointed, presidential encouragement, and faculty support and participation, the process of creating an academic and logistic structure began. The School of

International Studies (SIS) provided the opportunity to examine the university's centralization of various international programs. The SIS would be housed in Wes Watkins Center for International Trade and Development. This would allow adequate space for centralization of these international programs along with the Graduate Studies program, operating in accordance with the original USDA agreement regarding the use of the Wes Watkins Center. Plans would also begin in program promotion and graduate student recruitment.

Dedication Service

The formal dedication service for the School of International Studies was held on April 1, 1999.[39] A number of OSU staff, faculty, students, honored guests and friends gathered to commemorate this historic occasion. Among the OSU official representatives participating in the programs were President James Halligan, Dean James Hromas, OSU Executive Vice President Marvin Keener, OSU Associate Professor Emeritus Conrad Evans, OSU Board of Regents Chairman Jack Givens, OSU Director of International Business Programs Stephen Miller and OSU Division of Agriculture Assistant Dean for International Programs James Osborn. Among the honored guests were Congressman Wes Watkins, Peace Corps Regional Manager Morris Baker, Oklahoma Lieutenant Governor Mary Fallin, Member of Scotland's Parliament Henry McLeish and Oklahoma State Chamber President and CEO, Richard Rush. Two other very special guests were Judge Tom Bennett (son of Henry Garland Bennett) and Ben Hardy III (son of Benjamin Hardy II).[40] Although their distinguished fathers died together during Point Four service in the plane crash in Iran in 1951, the two had never met until this ceremony.

The ceremonies were in conjunction with the Wes Watkins Distinguished Lectureship featuring Mike Copps, assistant secretary for trade development, U. S. Department of Commerce. The presentation of the School of International Studies was given by OSU Chairman of the Board of Regents, Jack Givens. He stated, "With the establishment of the School, OSU reaffirmed its commitment to provide a university-wide focus for international academics." He added, "Through your collective efforts, educational opportunities and experiences will be created to challenge all to become not only locally concerned but fully participating global citizens."[41] The official mission of the SIS was "to provide a university-wide focus to energize and expand international opportunities in instruction, research, and extension for individuals and organizations seeking a greater understanding and involvement in world trade and international affairs."[42] With the official establishment of the SIS, a wonderful new facility, strong leadership and university support, the time for development and definition was to begin.

Development of the School of International Studies

Within the university, seven areas of study had agreed to cooperate in the programs of the School of International Studies (SIS). These are the College of Agricultural Sciences and Natural Resources, College of Education, College of Arts and Sciences, College of Engineering, Architecture and Technology, Graduate College, College of Business Administration and the College of Human Environmental Services. A board of directors was created with the deans of these academic colleges, the deans of the Graduate College and UEIED. This would become known as the SIS Deans' Administrative Committee. Within the SIS itself, several university programs were incorporated. Additional international programs would be created over the next decade. An examination of these SIS programs can best be seen by the success stories of participating students.

[This section of the SIS story will deal with the first ten years of the programs. Statistics and leadership references relate to that time period. More current data will be provided in the third section of this book.]

Program Developments

There were several important programs already in existence on campus that would find better operating identity under the umbrella of the SIS. These programs were the English Language Institute, Study Abroad, Peace Corps Recruiting, Graduate Program and Outreach.

English Language Institute

The English Language Institute (ELI) is the oldest continuous part of the SIS structure. It was created in the summer of 1970 in the foreign language department. The program was administered by William S. Abbott and was eventually placed under the Office of International Programs. From its beginning, there has been one continuous leader, Kay Woodruff Keys. In 1976, Keys and Jeanne Horton served as co-directors. In 1988, Keys was named as director, with all administrative and academic responsibilities. She brought to the institute administrative skills that have allowed the program to continually grow in its outreach and effectiveness. The program continues to be financially self-supporting through private contract and renewed contract agreements with international universities and organizations for instruction in English language skills. There is usually a 50-50 mix of family versus other sponsorships. Student ages range from 18 to 50 years of age with older career professionals returning to get their doctorate degrees. The ELI is defined as "an intensive program designed to assist non-native English speakers achieve the level of English proficiency necessary to begin their studies at the university level and is suitable for individuals who wish to learn English for business or personal reasons." In 1983 the ELI became a part of the University and College Intensive English Programs (UCIEP), a prestigious consortium of colleges administering English programs. The ELI was the host headquarters (central office) for the UCIEP from 1995-2000.

The 2009 annual report revealed that among the 231 enrollees are students from 22 countries which include Bahrain, Belarus, Brazil, Burkina Faso, China, Colombia, Honduras, Indonesia, Iran, Iraq, Japan, Korea, Libya, Mali, Oman, Saudi Arabia, Taiwan/ROC, Thailand, Turkey, United States and Vietnam.

In its over forty years of service, the ELI has many outstanding achievements. The evidence of continued contract renewals speaks well of its reputation and effectiveness. The very high percentage of students meeting language proficiency and matriculating in undergraduate programs, also gives testimony to the program's accomplishments. Although many statistics can bear evidence of great achievements, nothing can speak higher than personal illustrations. One Japanese student, completing the program, went on to become a successful businessman. In gratitude for ELI's significance in his success, the student returned to the OSU campus twenty years later to present a check for $25,000 to the ELI. The program has been in existence long enough that parents who went through the program as students now bring their children for that same language education at OSU.[43]

Mentioned in the introduction of this book was Diego Alvarez. His professional experiences since graduation were noted, but the significance of his relationship with the ELI program was essential to his successes. He came to the program with no level of understanding English. Alvarez stated "Learning English at ELI-OSU was an amazing experience, it opened a new world for me. At all levels. And it has not ended." One of the most valuable lessons Alvarez learned at the ELI and SIS was discovering "cultural differences... sharing with students from different countries is on the top of the list. So many countries that you may never visit ever, but that through people you have an idea of their lifestyles." He is considering the possibility of returning to ELI-OSU for a short-term course to keep up his English skills.[44]

Kevin Fisher worked as an undergraduate for two years as a student conversation leader in the English Language Institute. He completed his undergraduate work with majors in Political Science and German. He then joined the inaugural class of the SIS Graduate Program. He did his internship at the U. S. State Department's International Aviation Programs and Policy office. He also worked as a legislative assistant to Oklahoma Representative Wes Watkins. For the last seven years Fisher has worked as a manager for American Airlines Government Affairs Office where he is a part of AA's expansion in Europe and China. Fisher informs us, "In my job, I inform members of Congress and their staff about this issue and solicit their support for liberalizing trade in international aviation." He summarizes, "The SIS Program's interdisciplinary program prepared me to perform my job successfully, as I am required to possess advanced knowledge and experience in several areas, using that for the benefit of my company."[45]

Study Abroad

Before the official campus creation of the Study Abroad/National Student Exchange Office, most of the study abroad activities were grouped under the Global Studies activities in the College of Arts and Sciences. The Study Abroad Office opened in 1996 under the Office of International Programs. It was later placed under the SIS. Since its opening, the office increased from one professional staff member to three and added trained student peer advisors to handle the recruiting and advising load, as well as a graduate assistant from the School of International Studies. The mission of the Study Abroad program is to facilitate "students' participation in study, internship, or volunteer opportunities abroad." The office coordinates reciprocal exchanges, the National Student Exchange, and affiliated/approved programs and promotes study abroad campus-wide. The program was directed by Gerry Auel.

Both short-term and long-term study opportunities are assisted with national, private and university scholarships. The OSU provost provided funding for an incentive grant program that grew from $40,000 in 2006 to $150,000 in 2008. The grant is administered through the Study Abroad/National Student Exchange Office. The total funding from OSU sources was over $350,000 in 2008.

Campus-wide interest in study abroad was expressed in a 2008 recommendation from the Faculty Council and approved by the OSU Regents that suggests the university set a goal of having 25 percent of its graduates participating in a significant international experience, with an over-arching goal of 100 percent participation.[46] The recommendation resulted in increased focus on international education. Participation in credit-bearing study abroad activities grew from 302 in 2000 to 487 in 2009, representing approximately 2 percent of the total student body. Short-term faculty-led programs account for almost 70 percent of the study abroad participation numbers. Keeping true to the foundation of a land-grant university, the College of Agriculture Sciences and Natural Resources is at the forefront of the study abroad and exchange opportunities.

While a unit of the SIS, the Study Abroad/National Student Exchange Office is housed in the Student Union near other student services. Adjacent to the Study Abroad office is the Office of International Students and Scholars. Reporting to the Vice President for Student Affairs, the ISS serves international students and scholars, not only in compliance with immigration, but also in recruiting and programming for international students. Directing this program is Tim Huff. A new initiative at OSU is the Study Abroad House.

Located in the traditional Kerr-Drummond Residence Hall, it offers the opportunity for international and U. S. students to interact in a "learning community," to increase cultural understanding and to assist in the integration of international students in to the life of the campus.[47]

Additional statistics and historical events could be presented, but the real impact of this program as in other international programs is seen in people- adventurous students who sought to broaden their worldview, enhance their cultural competence, and increase their ability to contribute to the global community. Ryan Pardee studied in Zaragosa, Spain, the spring semester, 1998. Besides sharpening his Spanish-speaking skills, Pardee's cultural understanding grew from living in a very different culture. After graduation from OSU, Ryan joined the Federal Bureau of Investigation (FBI) where he worked in Washington, D. C. as an agent investigating both violent and drug crimes. His knowledge of Spanish has been very helpful in investigative experiences. Pardee sums up the value of his study abroad experiences as follows: "It is impossible in today's globally burgeoning economy to understand the complex, governmental, and societal intricacies without first hand knowledge of how these are affected by everyday life."[48]

Blake Lowry's study abroad experience at the Charles Darwin University in Darwin, Australia, in the spring of 2004 on a recipro-cal exchange program. Upon completion of his master's degree in accounting at OSU, Lowry has had the opportunity for additional foreign travel as well as extensive domestic travel. He worked for Conocco-Phillips as an external auditor and continues with travels taking him to Norway, Australia, Singapore, England and Canada. Lowry is very positive about the value of his college study abroad experience. He states, "My experience abroad has played a role in my educational pursuits by giving me a fuller education and expos-ing me to experiences and places I would not have otherwise had the opportunity to observe... the things I learned while studying away are sure to help me in my future professional career and personal life."[49]

Gemma Hughes experienced study abroad from a different perspective. From August 2004, through May 2005, Hughes left England to study at OSU. She spent her time at OSU conducting research for her undergraduate dissertation and returned to complete her degree plan at the University of Leicester in the summer, 2006. Her career plan includes involvement in British politics. Hughes indicated that her study abroad experience, "has broadened my outlook on life to no end and has really made me appreciate other cultures that I came into contact with, not just Americans but people from all over Europe and the world who were also international students."[50]

Lauren C. Manners has had extensive experiences in study abroad. Manners studied at the University of Hertfordshire as an OSU reciprocal exchange student 2001-2002. She continued studies at the University of Oxford in the OSU Scholar Development Program in the summer of 2003. She worked in an internship at the American Embassy in London during the summer of 2004. Upon completion of the bachelor's degree at OSU, she received a master's degree with distinction from a prestigious London school of business. She began a career in Washington, D. C. with the U. S. government as a proliferation analyst. Manners confessed that her study abroad experiences exemplified, "some of the hardest years of my life as I came to know who I was and what I believed in and what I was capable when I was out in the world on my own. I am certainly able to be related to a lot more people in this world and have a different outlook on life than before I studied abroad." Manners added that, "I would never have discovered my passion for the international world. I am now looking forward to a career dealing with international situations on a daily basis and international travel."[51]

Nana Honda came to OSU from Japan in 1999 and continued her studies until 2003. She met another student from France and they married. She worked for a year as an international student advisor in Florida. With her husband in France, she recalled, "The university is wonderful place to study because I had the opportunity to meet different individuals from all over the world—not only academically but socially and culturally." She adds, "The studying abroad experience gave the urge and the passion to want to help out students from different countries myself."[52]

Anne-Charlotte Sequeval came to OSU from France for the 2002-2003 school year as a reciprocal exchange student. She served as an accountant for Michelin Services in the United Kingdom. Sequeval relates that, "I am working in a company where there are 24 nationalities and it was very easy to integrate this team when I arrived. I am very open-minded to the different cultures and I enjoy speaking in English." She summed up her study abroad experiences by saying, "Studying abroad was an unique and excellent experience. Living with different people, studying in another language, make you grow up."[53]

Benjamin Prentice is a graduate of the SIS program has served in Washington, D. C. as a staff assistant for the International Foundation for Electoral Systems (IFES) and as an ESL Instructor, inlingua, in Arlington, Virginia. He began his academic international interest with a declared major at OSU in political science and international relations. He studied Russian language. He was able to receive two prestigious scholarships for a study abroad in St. Petersburg, Russia. After completion of an master's degree in the OSU School of International Studies, he returned to Russia to teach English. Benjamin stated, "Now I work for an international non-profit organization dealing with democracy development and election assistance, as well as teaching English to foreign professionals in the Washington, D. C. area. I should be starting a career with the National Geospatial-Intelligence Agency as a regional analyst." Benjamin related in expressive words his evaluation of the study abroad experience stating, "I am part of something much larger—a tapestry of brilliant colors and vibrant cultures that must be explored and appreciated. We have one chance on this planet—don't waste it nestled away in the cocoon of your hometown or preconceived notions about the world."[54]

Brian Tran studied abroad in Lund, Sweden in 2003. His experience in Europe caused him to love the international encounters and motivated him to enter the SIS Graduate Program. He graduated from SIS in May 2006, with an master's degree in International Studies with a focus on International Business and Economic Relations. He worked in business in Southern California. His international experience has taught him, "the world is a big place but it's filled with good people. We all have our differences but it's petty compared to the real problems that face our society such as hunger and disease."[55]

Several other study abroad students have gone on to pursue advanced degrees. Bryan and Katie Thomason experienced a study abroad opportunity in the spring of 2004 at the University of Hertfordshire in the United Kingdom. Bryan pursued a doctoral degree in seminary and Katie completed a law degree at Harvard Law in Massachusetts. Their time abroad gave them the confidence they needed to pursue these advanced degrees. They stated, "We've experienced some of the world, but this has made us want to go further, to see and experience more." Christian Lenckner came to OSU from Germany for the 2004-2005 school year. He finished his graduate studies in Bamberg, Germany. He stated, "Ever since I returned to Germany I've been trying to add more international experiences to my agenda, e.g. mentoring for incoming exchange students here in Bamberg, attending language courses in Spain or organizing internships abroad." He has considered returning to the United States to add a second master's degree.[56]

Whether participating in long-term or short-term programs, participants agree that the experience broadens their worldview and widens their perspectives. The StudyAbroad/National Student Exchange Office is instrumental in facilitating students' desire to become more independent and to better understand the world in which they live today. In today's climate of global interaction, the ability to appreciate and interact with persons from different cultures has become an essential part of a well-rounded education.

Peace Corps Recruiting

With the creation of the Peace Corps under President John F. Kennedy in 1961, college campuses have been a natural source for recruitment. There was serious consideration in Congress of naming the Peace Corps after Henry Bennett because of his outstanding leadership in the Point Four program a decade earlier.[57] With the historical commitment of OSU to international technical assistance, the Peace Corps was an ideal program well suited to the campus. Another unique connection with OSU and the Peace Corps was found in Vera Preston-Jaeger. She is the granddaughter of Henry and Vera Bennett. A 1962 graduate of OSU, she was one of the earliest volunteers who served in the Peace Corps in Ecuador from 1962 through 1964.[58] Since the Peace Corps' creation, the OSU campus, as of 2009, witnessed 458 alumni serving throughout the world.

The Peace Corps Recruitment Office was established on campus in 2003. Its purpose was to "promote international opportunities for OSU, Langston University, and the surrounding area." Recent national changes in the Peace Corps program necessitated the main recruitment responsibility to move to a central independent office in Dallas, Texas, in October of 2008. But OSU is still actively seeking to involve its graduates in the Peace Corps opportunities under the SIS. A master's level degree in international studies, called the Masters International Program, is also possible through Peace Corps experience. Examples of the Peace Corps experiences indicate the far-reaching impact it continues to have on the SIS graduates.[59]

Cajuan Theard began his international experiences as a participant in the OSU study abroad program in 2003 going to the Sampere Language School and Suffolk University Madrid campus in Spain. He stated, "My travels have not only allowed me to appreciate the customs and cultures of many people across the world but also allowed me to have a greater appreciation for the customs and culture of my own country." He went on to serve as a Peace Corps volunteer in the Dominican Republic.[60]

Noah Domnick is a 2008 SIS graduate. Coming from a family of OSU loyalists, he was well prepared for the campus experience. He did undergraduate work with degrees in Spanish and psychology. With a strong interest in the Peace Corps, he was immediately interested in the SIS Graduate Program incorporating the Peace Corps experience. He served in Piura, Peru, and now works for the U. S. Department of Justice. Domnick states, "some valuable lessons I learned at SIS was to take advantage of the rich diversity of students the program offers. The classroom was a representation of members of different countries from across the globe." He discovered the value of flexibility and open-mindedness in the workplace. His long-term goals for applying his SIS education includes "improving my second language fluency, continuing international education, and making tangible improvements to the way we look into solving future global issues." In the summer of 2009, Noah was married to Liz Howard, a May 2009 graduate of the SIS Graduate Program and administrative assistant to Dr. James Hromas. Noah has used his language skills as an FBI agent.[61]

A different approach regarding this international program is seen in Samantha Wolthuis. She had served in the Peace Corps in Uzbekistan. While working in Tulsa, Oklahoma, she began to search for an Uzbek community in the states. She became aware of some Uzbek students attending OSU and entered the SIS graduate program. While there she was able to participate in an International Women's Conference in Abu Dhabi, United Arab Emirates. The experience was very rewarding and valuable personal and professional contacts were made. Wolthuis completed her master's degree at SIS in December 2006. She worked as associate director of the American Jewish World Service. In that capacity Wolthuis carries on the OSU legacy of Henry Bennett and Point Four. Wolthuis explains that in her job she "sends individuals (primarily Americans) to lend technical assistance and support to the staff of NGOs in Africa, Asia, and the Americas." She also expresses the hopes of "running a Peace Corps country office in the developing world in five years."[62]

In addition to the three existing programs placed under the SIS organization, new and exciting programs were created to enhance the international study experiences. These programs are the Graduate Certificate Program, the International Outreach Unit, the OSU-Mexico Liaison Office, the Fulbright Resource Center and the Phi Beta Delta International Society.

Graduate Program

At the heart of the SIS is the Graduate Program. It gives the SIS its distinctive identity and academic base. Led by a director and graduate program committee, the program finds its real strength and lifeblood in the volunteer efforts of over 140 faculty members in the various colleges of the university. In the fall of 2009, ninety students entered the international studies program. Among these were thirty-five international students and fifty-five domestic students. The five focus areas are International Human Relations, Society & Education, International Business & Economic Relations, International Trade & Development and Preservation of Cultural & Ecological Resources.[63]

Three options are offered in the multi-disciplinary masters program: the Masters of Science in International Studies, the Masters in International Programs and the Certificate of International Studies. The first program director was Maureen J. Nemecek followed by Nancy Wilkinson. The Graduate Program was directed by Stephen Miller. Donna Birchler, first known as administrative assistant and now as the program's Graduate Advisor, has been with the program as administrative assistant from its beginning. Since its initiation in 1999, 229 students have graduated with masters degrees. Of these graduates, 111 are from 43 countries and 118 are from 22 states. Currently there are SIS graduate students from 23 countries and 14 U. S. states.[64] Several distinguished fellowships are awarded to selected outstanding Graduate Program students: The Lawrence L. Boger Distinguished Graduate Fellowship, the Wes and Lou Watkins Distinguished Graduate Fellowship, the Les Martin Endowed Graduate Fellowship and the James D. White Endowed Graduate Fellowship. The James G. Hromas Distinguished Graduate Fellowship was awarded beginning in 2010. Internships within the Graduate Program are sponsored by the Michael S. Hyatt Fellowship, the Boeing Company and Spirit, Inc.[65]

A number of student success stories are unfolding for the graduates of the SIS Grauate Study program. An early graduate of this program is Andrew Golembiewski. He worked as a detective in San Diego, California. In 1995 Golembiewski was a star football player in California. He was offered a football scholarship at OSU. He left

Wes and Lou Watkins (center) with scholarship recipients.

the fast-paced life of the west coast to pursue his studies in the relative calmness of Oklahoma. He found a very friendly and helpful campus community. In addition to the disciplined football regimen, Golembiewski earned excellent academic standing. His academic advisor suggested that he consider the graduate program of the new School of International Studies (SIS). With his strong academic background, it was thought that he should be able to complete the SIS master's program in a shorter time than expected. His greatest educational benefit in the SIS was his contact and encounters with the many different cultures represented. He was among the first graduates of the SIS in July 2000, and he graduated with a 4.0 grade point average. Upon completion of the degree program, Andrew returned to San Diego and began work in the police department. He has worked as a patrolman, an investigator and even in undercover endeavors. His experiences at SIS greatly aided him working in a very multi-cultural community. He has high praise for the SIS program and staff.[66]

Gi-son Jeon is from South Korea. In December 2000, he enrolled in the SIS Graduate Program. He wanted to improve in his work regarding cultural properties care and management through the multi-cultural experiences offered by the program. The experiences at the SIS helped him to hold a wider viewpoint of the world through interaction with the other international students on various subject matters of interest to him, such as tourism and park management. On return to South Korea, he was promoted to senior management. He was motivated to do additional study and received a Ph. D. from Soong-sil University in Seoul. He worked as a senior museum educator in the National Park Museum of Korea Department of Exhibition and Promotion. He has held a part-time professor position at a university in Seoul since 2007.[67]

Matt Henson graduated from the SIS Graduate Program in July 2005. In the program he worked as a graduate assistant on the OKSource program to develop a business platform facilitating Oklahoma exports. For his internship he worked with the U. S. Department of Commerce's Inland Empire U. S. Export Assistance Center (USEAC). He focused on assisting small and medium-sized companies in exportation. Following graduation, Henson worked at the International Traffic in Arms Regulations (ITAR) and Export Administration Regulations (EAR) as a contractor for a Los Angeles defense company. After two years he joined a similar company in Indiana. There he has worked on an electronic export management software (similar to his OKSource experiences) and was promoted to Manager of Trade Automation. He worked to standardize and automate common trade compliance activities across the company. He states, "My job is to enable compliant trade in a world where global market imperatives are driving companies to seek new markets, lower cost inputs and new technologies and global security imperatives are causing governments to add to an already complicated global regulatory environment."[68]

Stephanie Fox chose to come to OSU because of the combination of the College of Agriculture and the SIS. She completed the SIS Graduate Program in May 2005. She works with the North Dakota Department of Agriculture. She relates, "I work with people from all walks of life, people from many different countries, and in my travels I have been able to apply lessons learned from my friends at SIS. Everything from cultural mannerisms to languages to things I learned in my classes and people I met along the way." Fox's long-term goals are "to continue working in agriculture on an international level, helping to provide quality food to destinations around the globe and helping to educate people in the necessary benefits and important role agriculture plays in all cultures and countries." Henry Bennett would be so proud of this continuing purpose![69]

Stuart Barnes grew up in a totally OSU environment. He developed a strong interest in American foreign policy and entered OSU with a major in political science. Upon his completion of a bachelor's degree, he was encouraged by his professors to consider the new SIS program. He found a great opportunity to expand on his undergraduate degree. Barnes expressed, "I learned cross cultural communication not just through course work but also through the experiences shared with the cadre of International students that SIS attracts." Barnes completed his SIS master's program in May 2003. He now serves as a civil affairs officer with the Army reserves. Barnes found his SIS experience very useful in "understanding how to communicate and empathize with leaders from differing cultural backgrounds and political motivations in Iraq and Afghanistan…" Barnes confesses, "My education from SIS may have saved my skin a time or two, as my knowledge and experience were primary weapons in our fight against terrorism and religious extremism." Barnes looks ahead to the continued value of his SIS education. He states, "My SIS education and experience will only continue to provide me with the tools and abilities to react to, and be engaged in, the ever-changing world of geopolitics."[70]

Elsa Velasco came to OSU from Venezuela. There was already familiarity with the university as her parents and brothers had attended. She was very interested in international studies, but could not find the "right mix" until she discovered the OSU School of International Studies. She completed her degree in May 2006. She learned from her SIS experience to "Embrace your differences. Once we learn this, understanding and tolerance comes through." Velasco worked as "the international sales person in a public company that deals on a regular basis with many complex compliance and sales issues." She encouraged her brother to enter the SIS program. He graduated in 2008. Velasco says, "I very much look forward to going back for the Ph.D.- when it becomes an option."[71]

Ajay Aluri, from India, completed her Graduate Program requirement at the SIS in December 2007. Aluri described his feelings about the SIS Graduate Program in the following words:

> When I think about the International Studies program in OSU, I can recollect a famous quote from Ralph Waldo Emerson, 'Do not go where the path may lead; go instead where there is no path and leave a trail.' The International Studies program is designed to provide opportunities that fit the diverse interests of students and to pursue quality learning in various focus areas. This multi-disciplinary program not only facilitated me to find a new path in my career but also provided and international exposure and experience. Through this program, I was able to reach my goal and to continue my advanced academic studies as a doctoral student in Hospitality Management.[72]

Martin Kanjadza graduated from the SIS in May 2005. Several universities with international study programs were considered. Personal and prompt attention from the SIS staff, plus a generous assistantship, made OSU the best choice. In the program Kanjadza "came out a global citizen." Extensive international travel and experience opportunities allowed him to become an advocate for international education. Kanjadza has hopes of becoming a legislator in his home in Malawi.[73]

One of the significant graduates of the SIS Graduate Program is Abenet Yemenu. He is from Ethiopia and graduated in December 2003. His father graduated from the Jimma and Alemaya schools that were established by the Oklahoma A & M faculty and staff in the 1950s. Although his father did not attend OSU, his son did find his way to OSU. It is an interesting connection of Henry Bennett's early ties and commitments to Ethiopian Emperor Halie Selassie that fifty years later the son of an Ethiopian native would be a graduate of the OSU School of International Studies.[74]

International Outreach Unit

The purposes of the International Outreach Unit (IOU) are threefold: to bring internationally respected speakers to OSU for the Wes Watkins Distinguished Lectureship and the Global Briefing Series; to promote international education, research, trade and outreach on behalf of OSU and Oklahoma, and; to serve as an international resource center to support the needs of the university and public and private sectors, both locally and globally.[75] Among those guest speakers were Dr. Duck-Woo Nam, Harriet Mayor Fulbright, Dr. Adan Badran and Steve Forbes.

The Wes Watkins Distinguished Lectureship, generously funded by Lou and Wes Watkins, has become a popular campus event with outstanding speakers of national and international acclaim. The Global Briefing Series attracts leaders with international areas of expertise to provide information and dialogue of current interests. Through the IOU, OSU has active Memoranda of Understanding with 180 universities in sixty countries opening doors for mutual exchange and opportunities for study abroad. The IOU also hosted several MOU signings each year. The IOU also tracks OSU involvement via the international travel database and the international activities database.

An important role for the IOU was the network of Global Contacts to discover possible sources of funding for the IOU programs. Private funding has been created by the Ambassadors Program to be given through the OSU Foundation. The Ambassadors also advised on keeping the SIS relevant and aware of national and international trends that may impact the SIS programs and personnel. In addition, the Ambassadors served as catalysts for individuals, organizations, institutions and businesses with interest in international opportunities in instruction, research, outreach, world trade and international affairs. Their activity has diminished over the last several years.

The Henry G. Bennett Distinguished Fellow Program was established to recognize those individuals who have made outstanding contributions to the finding solutions to global issues, like Dr. Bennett. Those selected serve as intellectual assets to SIS and OSU through their fields of expertise in academe, business, government, media and the non-profit sector. In honor of the contributions made by President Boger, he was acknowledged as the first recipient of the Henry G. Bennett Distinguished Fellows program. Following his death, a Graduate Distinguished Fellowship was named in his honor. Dr. Richard C. Poole, OSU Dean and Vice President Emeritus agreed to lead a fundraising effort for a $500,000 professorship of International studies in Boger's name that was completed in 2007.

Serving as the OSU International Education and Outreach Global Contacts Coordinator is Jim C. Shideler. Coming from a background as a financial analyst and accountant for Armstrong World Industries and OSU Human Environmental Sciences, Shideler has coordinated efforts to build new alliances with businesses, organizations and private partners that can advance IE&O's mission and support students in the department. He prides himself on helping IE&O "build a reputation for excellence, maintaining our goal of service to facilitate and expand interdisciplinary international opportunities in instruction, research and outreach; sustaining global engagements."[76]

An example of the SIS student involvement in affecting Oklahoma globalization is seen in Eleanor Inglis. She was a non-traditional graduate student beginning her SIS studies eleven years after her undergraduate degree. For her the SIS experience values "were all the international perspectives, opinions, ideas, and ways of the world... sitting in class with classmates from Africa, Central America, India, and Asia allowed me to understand world events through the eyes of its global citizens." Inglis graduated from SIS with her master's degree in December 2002. She served as the director of international education at Oklahoma City University. A close working relationship is maintained with the OSU School of International Studies. Inglis states, "If I could somehow affect Oklahoma's globalization effort, if I could bring the world to

Oklahomans, then I would have done something of value in my life."[77]

OSU-Mexico Liaison Office

The OSU-Mexico Liaison Office (MLO) began operation in 2006 for the purposes of promoting bilateral exchange between the United States and Mexico through an increase of the number of Mexican students enrolled at OSU and the number of OSU students studying abroad in Mexico. The MLO, begun under the direction of Jose Sagarnaga, assists faculty and staff in facilitating the MLO purposes and general international program support. Since the programs inception, a number of distinguished experts on U.S.-Mexican relations have graced the OSU campus as guest speakers. Among these were Former Policy advisor for President Clinton's Special Envoy for the Americas, Ana Maria Salazar; Oklahoma Hispanic Chamber of Commerce President, Xavier Neira, and; former President of Mexico, Vicente Fox, who visited Oklahoma at the invitation of the Spears School of Business and received the Henry G. Bennett Distinguished Fellow Award. Activities have been established with educational institutions in the Mexican States of Puebla and Chihuahua. There have been numerous students and faculty trips to Mexico and new programs to bring Mexican students to the U. S. each year.

MLO student success stories can be illustrated by the experiences of Fernando Jimenez-Arevalo. He credits Dr. James Hromas with the beginning of the cooperative relationship with OSU and Universidad Autonoma del Estado de Mexico (UAEM). Gerry Auel and Eleanor Inglis went on a recruiting trip to Toluva and met with Jimenez. He was approved for a study program at OSU. He took business classes and found an advisor and friend in business college faculty member Dr. Kevin E. Voss. Jimenez progressed well and entered the SIS Graduate Program where he also served as president of the Student Association for Global Affairs (SAGA). He participated in global debates and competitions representing the SIS. Following his master's degree at SIS, Jimenez was encouraged to continue in a College of Business Ph. D. program at OSU. Jimenez completed his doctoral program in 2009. His hope was to return to Mexico and teach at UAEM. The university was unable to provide the desired position, but Jimenez found employment with the University of Texas at El Paso where he was able to educate other Hispanic students in business pursuits who daily cross the U. S. -Mexican border. Jimenez expresses his appreciation for "UAEM, the SIS and the College of Business for giving me the opportunity to become a better professional, improve my family, and my countrymen."[78]

Fulbright Resource Center

The Fulbright Center providing support and guidance for Fulbright Grant initiatives is housed within the School of International Studies. Named after the late Arkansas Senator J. William Fulbright, the grant program funds international activities including lecturing and/or research for faculty and professionals and as well as graduate study, research, or English Teaching Assistantships for graduating seniors and graduate students. Senator Fulbright proposed the legislation founding the program to promote "mutual understanding between the people of the United States and the people of other countries of the world."[79] It has been described as one of the most successful U. S. initiatives to foster global understanding.

Working with the Study Abroad Office and Fulbright Advisor, Steve Hallgren, the Fulbright Resource Center is dedicated to assisting students in a competitive application and completing the campus interview process for the Fulbright U. S. Student Program. With the establishment of the Fulbright Resource Center, the presence of a Fulbright Program Advisor who is a faculty member, and the full support of the OSU Provost who sponsors an annual reception for Fulbright Scholars, the office has increased visibility of the Fulbright program on campus. This as resulted in increasing numbers of scholarships and grants being awarded to OSU students and faculty.

In the 2008-2009 academic year, OSU produced thirteen applications for national review of which three were accepted for English Teaching Assistant awards to Indonesia, Mexico and Korea. In addition, two OSU faculty members were awarded Fulbright Senior Scholar awards to Turkey and Belgium. Two other OSU faculty members will complete Fulbright Specialist assignments in Slovenia.[80]

Phi Beta Delta Honor Society for International Students

The Phi Beta Delta Honor Society is a prestigious honor society for international scholars. It is the first honor society dedicated to recognize scholarly achievement in international education. The OSU Epsilon Upsilon charter was established in 2004 and is coordinated by a professional staff member within the School of International Studies. Membership renewal dues fund a scholarship to help students to attend conferences with an international focus. By 2009, the chapter had inducted 162 members, including 24 honorary members.[81]

International Commitments and Program Cooperation

Since the establishment of the SIS in 1999, there have been continued international commitments through the university colleges. International agreements have grown between OSU and fifty-seven countries in those ten years. Among these are Argentina (2), Australia (2), Belize (1), Botswana (1), Brazil (9), Canada (4), China (13), Colombia (2), Costa Rica (5), Czech Republic (1), Denmark (2), Egypt (1), England (6), Ethiopia (9), Finland (2), France (1), Georgia (1), Germany (5), Greece (1), Honduras (1), Iceland (1), India (6), Indonesia (2), Iraq (2), Ireland (1), Italy (7), Jamaica (1), Japan (6), Jordan (3), Kazakhstan (1), Kenya (2), Libya (1), Lithuania (1), Malaysia (1), Mali (1), Mexico (32), Mongolia (1), Mozambique (4), Netherlands (2), Norway (1), Philippines (3), Puerto Rico (1), Russia (1), Scotland (1), Sierra Leone (1), Singapore (1), Slovakia (1), South Africa (2), South Korea (11), Spain (1), Switzerland (1), Taiwan (1), Thailand (11), Turkey (3), Ukraine (1), United Arab Emirates (5) and Vietnam (5). The significance and secret to the SIS success is the cooperation among the various programs and colleges of the university. Combined with a centralized history and presenting accounting credibility, the process offers potential growth in international services for the university.[82]

Five-Year Anniversary

On April 8, 2004, the School of International Studies com-memorated its first five years of service to the university and the international community. The event signified the SIS's purpose of serving "as an academic framework for integrating OSU colleges' international resources." The School of Veterinary Medicine be-came the eighth university college to join the SIS interdisciplinary study. Reports were given of important events during those five years. On October 6, 2000, the Point Four Room was created in the Wes Watkins Center with an Ethiopian motif and numerous histori-cal displays of the Oklahoma A & M- Ethiopia connections. A re-union of OSU Point Four workers were gathered there and honored for their service.[83]

Ten-Year Anniversary

On April 9, 2009, the SIS celebrated ten years of international service with a special program that coincided with the Wes Watkins Distinguished Lectureship delivered by Dr. Adnan Badran, former prime minister of Jordan and president of the University of Petra. Dr. Badran was a graduate of the OSU College of Agricultural Sci-ences and Natural Resources. Events of the day began with a recep-tion for the Honorable Tsutomu Osawa, Consul-General of Japan. A luncheon provided the occasion for presentations of scholarships and awards, followed by the guest lecture. Following the lecture, Henry G. Bennett Distinguished Fellow awards were presented to James E. Halligan, Michael S. Hyatt and Adnan Badran. In the af-ternoon, three Global Awareness panels made the presentations on Economy, Foreign Policy and Africa, with questions from the public following. The panel on "Economy" was led by Michael Hyatt, Barry Clark, Brady Sidwell and Larry Sanders. The panel on "For-eign Policy" was led by Adnan Badran, Oleg Kravchenko, Tarana Mahmudova and Vigen Gabrielyan. The panel on "Africa" was led by Ambassador Abdoulaye Diop, Filipe Couto, Rogerio Uthui and Jason Kirksey. Following the panel, there was a dedication cer-emony of the Wes Watkins Center Global Plaza in honor of Wes and Lou Watkins. The presentation was made by Dr. James Hromas.[84]

Former Congressman Wes Watkins and Adnan Badran, former Prime Minister of Jordan at the 10-year Celebration.

Richard Poole and Brady Sidwell at the 10-year Celebration.

Funding

The Wes Watkins Center developed a master plan to raise money for student scholarships, professorships, fellowships and Chairs for the School of International Studies. The first endowed Chair, the Wes and Lou Watkins Endowed Chair also claims the name of the congressman and economic development supporter. The first professorship is named the Lawrence L. Boger Distinguished Professorship for the former OSU President recognizing his major contribution to raising the need for international education on campus. Richard W. Poole was highly instrumental in raising funds for the Boger Professorship working through until the goal was met.[85]

Several scholarships and fellowships supporting the efforts of international education have been endowed. Professor B. Curtis Hamm led the effort to provide funding for the James G. Hromas Distinguished Graduate Fellowship that was funded from the International Education and Outreach staff as well as from family and friends. The Lawrence L. Boger Distinguished Graduate Fellowship is another honor for the former OSU president. This award, funded generously by his family, is given to one top student selected for advanced study and work in the international arena. The James D. White Agricultural Education Endowed Scholarship Fund came into being after the untimely death of Professor White. Recipients of this award are selected full-time students in the SIS who are pursuing an emphasis in agricultural trade and development.[86]

Another generous endowment was provided by Wes and Lou Watkins, the Wes and Lou Watkins Distinguished Graduate Fellowship, to assist a selected SIS student enrolled in the Master of Science program. The courtyard of the Wes Watkins Center is named in honor of Lou Watkins for both her financial contribution and her service to the university as a Regent and Board Chairperson. The Les Martin endowed Graduate Fellowship for a selected SIS student was also created by Wes and Lou Watkins in memory of and to honor Les Martin, an outstanding student killed in an auto accident. An established Wes and Lou Watkins Matthew 25:40 Endowed Scholarship Fund provides resources annually for four students to study abroad in underdeveloped countries addressing the issues of hunger, health, education and poverty.[87]

Michael S, Hyatt of Fort Worth, Texas, has generously funded the Michael S. Hyatt Graduate Intern Fellowship for a selected international student needing financial assistance. Previous recipients from Mexico and Ethiopia have had significant experience working with government and nonprofits in Washington, D.C. Mr. Hyatt continues to financially support the SIS program in other endeavors.[88]

The Boeing Company has generously supported a Graduate Internship for selected SIS students who have participated in significant summer internships in the U.S. Congress, American Airlines, Global Fund for Women, the United Nations Cargill Corporation, NATO and many other international organizations. One noteworthy example is Jose Sagarnaga, formerly of the OSU-Mexico Liaison Office in the SIS. Sagarnaga studied as a SIS graduate student with Nobel Laureate, Dr. Muhammad Yunus, Founder of the Grameen Bank in India. He studied the Micro-Banking and Finance impact of this successful program designed to help people break out of poverty and sustain economic growth.[89]

A Spirit AeroSystems Grant provides funds for selected SIS students with financial needs to travel overseas and domestically to participate in internships. Previous students have interned with the U.S. Department of State in Austria, Higher Education in Dubai U.A.E, Hudson Institute in Washington, D.C. and Children Service work in Taiwan.[90]

The Hugh Rouk Memorial Scholarship honors Hugh Rouk whose service in Ethiopia for OSU at Alemaya University was longer than any other OSU faculty or staff member. The fund assists selected graduates and faculty members of the Alemaya University of Agriculture in pursuit of a graduate degree or post-doctoral program at OSU. The Jud and Vera Milburn Endowed Fellowship in International Studies was created by Lynn Lansford to honor Jud Milburn, who served as long-time English professor at OSU and at the Alemaya University in Ethiopia. This annual fellowship goes to a selected post-baccalaureate student of Ethiopian nationality applying for admission as a full-time student in the SIS Graduate Program and has financial needs.[91]

The School of International Studies continues to pursue support from private and public donors in order to expand and further the goals of the SIS. OSU is fortunate to have the services of Dr. B. Curtis Hamm as a consultant and fundraiser for the university and the SIS programs. Dr. Hamm is Professor Emeritus of the Spear School of Business and Consultant to the OSU Foundation. He has numerous international education experiences in Europe and Asia including service as a Fulbright Professor in China and a USAID professor at the University of Jordan where he helped to begin their MBA program. He has been recognized for his international work by being selected for the National International Students Association Award. Dr. Hamm opened his heart to international needs by adopting a young Chinese boy while teaching in Zhongshan University. His son is now president of a successful business company in China.[92]

These anticipated funding avenues as well as newly discovered sources will help provide the resources for further development of the Oklahoma State University School of International Studies.

International Impacts

Over the years the SIS, like many other organizations, has been impacted by the events in the international community. To understand how these impacts affect Oklahoma State University and other organizations, we see further need for these types of global programs

With fall of the Berlin Wall and the collapse of the Soviet Empire, new relationships and opportunities came for international student recruitment and study abroad. With the emergence of new nation states from the former Soviet Bloc, new opportunities came for trade and training. Many of the new independent countries needed training for leaders in government, education and industry to be competitive in the world market. OSU would see an increased enrollment in students from these countries.

An often forgotten impact on the campus was the rapid decrease in the price of energy production. The oil-rich state of Oklahoma was dramatically affected by the drop in international oil prices that began in the late 1980s. This had an impact on state budgets and the state school's operating budgets. This required re-examination of their priorities and importance of less cost-effective programs.

The rapid increase in technology also had an important impact on the university's opportunities during this time. The availability of the personal computer and growth of the Internet gave an opportunity for increased communication and access to information.

This also provided an effective means of campus recruitment and marketing. The trend of campus national and international teleconferences offered more personal and inexpensive means of training and sharing of information.

With the emergence of the technological advances, globalization became another important influence on the OSU campus. The rapidly developing nations of India and China caused the traditional world powers to reconsider their understanding and practices of international trade. The developing new world powers saw the great need for educated workers and better trained workers with professional skills in international business. OSU benefited by having an increase in these international students needing teaching degrees and improved language skills. It also demonstrated the need for American students to be more attuned to international needs and relationships so that the United States could become more competitive in the global market.

International military conflicts and terrorist activities also affected the OSU international programs. Easing of tensions with Lybia saw an increase in the number of students from that country seeking an education. The growing conflict with Iraq led to an international coalition waging war on Iraq. Another generation of American soldiers were exposed to new international cultures and practices. Again, OSU students and families were made aware of international needs and opportunities that an OSU School of International Studies program could provide.

Part Three:

Learning and Looking Ahead: 2010 – present – future

"International Studies and Outreach's purpose is to serve as a resource for all of Oklahoma State University's academic units and colleges and to expand international opportunities in instruction, research and outreach for individuals and organizations seeking a greater understanding and involvement in world trade and international affairs. The future will provide many opportunities for OSU students, faculty and staff to internationalize – carrying on the vision of those who began this program many years ago. " (Dr. David M. Henneberry, Associate Vice President of the Division of International Studies and Outreach, April 2011)

"The world is a book and those who do not travel read only one page."
Saint Augustine, 425AD

SIS Development Since 2009

By the end of 2009 there had been much learned by the leadership about the challenges and mechanics of a strong, academically-oriented international program. Because the School of International Studies was a major part of a university system, there were also political and economic challenges to be faced. Major changes in the university's academic leadership directly affected the leadership of the SIS. Economic challenges for the university also created budget challenges for the SIS. With leadership and budget challenges, the opportunity for program evaluations and changes existed. With leadership, budget and program changes, new names and faces were seen.

Transition Period

During the early spring of 2009, major leadership changes and a period of transition were on the horizon for the SIS. In March 2010, Dr. James Hromas retired as director of the SIS. His ten years of leadership had allowed for the creation of a strong and nationally-recognized international studies program. The loss of his leadership and the vision he foresaw would have immediate impact on the SIS programs.

Dr. Hromas to Dr. Henneberry

An interim director of SIS was appointed by the outgoing provost. There were immediate changes in the organizational leadership and operation of the International Education and Outreach program. August 2010, Dr. David Henneberry, assistant dean of the College of Agriculture, was appointed the new interim director of the international outreach program. The university began a process to find a new director for the SIS program. After months of interviews from candidates across the country, a decision was made. The best possible candidate was found in one of OSU's own leadership. Dr. David Henneberry, assistant dean of the College of Agriculture, was selected and approved as Associate Vice President for International Studies and Outreach in April 2011. His familiarity with the creation and development of the SIS and his active participation on the SIS board allowed for his immediate and authoritative leadership. His past experience with international travel and contacts provided a smooth transition. The decision created renewed confidence among the SIS staff and related program leaders. He had already developed a good relationship with and had great respect for Dr. Hromas. He strongly encouraged Dr. Hromas's involvement in many of the program's activities. During his years of leadership, he has brought new insight into existing SIS programs and initiated new, needed programs and activities.

Department Leaders

In any time of university transition, there are those in leadership positions who evaluate their tenure of service. Such was the case in the months and years following the transition period. The Graduate Study program was directed by Stephen Miller. Upon his retirement, Joel Jenswold took over as director. The Study Abroad program had been led very capably for sixteen years by Gerry Auel. Upon her retirement in 2012, she returned to her great love in the Peace Corps. Jeff Simpson now leads the department. The Mexico Liaison programs were transferred from Jose Sagarnaga. Rodrigo Tello, who works with Alejandro Aizpuru in the UPAEP Liaison office and the ITESM office is waiting to be filled. The Fulbright Program is now under the directorship of Steve Hallgren. The English Language Institute saw the retirement of Kay Keys at the end of 2013 after a distinguished service as director for twenty-five years. Dr. Deborah Montgomery began her term as the director of ELI from January 2014 – January 2016 and Fred Griffiths' term began January 2016.[1]

Name Changes

Also in a time of transition, the program changes allowed for significant name changes. Some of these changes were forced upon the program and some were necessitated by the change in direction for a program. The International Education and Outreach (IE&O) was changed to International Study and Outreach (IS&O). The previous Graduate Study program of the SIS was changed to the Academic Programs office.

Major Events

After Dr. Henneberry assumed leadership of the SIS, there were many significant events. Among these were distinguished visitors and speakers, major donations received and new program expansions. Two of the internationally recognized speakers were the former Prime Minister of Great Britain, Tony Blair and former Secretary of Defense, Robert Gates. A series of documentaries on the Point Four programs, initiated by OSU in Ethiopia, was produced and previewed at the Wes Watkins Center by the creator, Mel Tewahade. A new National Guard training emphasis was created in the Correspondence Education program. Increased college involvement in the SIS program was seen in Tulsa campus engineering and the VetMed programs. Strategic partner offices were established with Monterry Tech, UPAEP and Southwest Jiaotong. Additional Memoranda of Understanding were created and are detailed later in this book. In the fall of 2013 Dr. James Hromas received the Henry G. Bennett Distinguished Fellow Award.[2]

Several outstanding donations were received to assist the international studies program. Don and Cathey Humphreys established a very generous scholarship program to assist OSU students in study abroad trips. Other contributions were given by Brady Sidwell, Mike Hyatt and the Farzaneh brothers – Jalal and Mohammad.

Don and Cathey Humphreys (center) and President Burns Harigs, and First Cowgirl Ann Hargis with Humphreys' scholarship recipients.

Jalal Farzaneh (left) and Mohammad Farzaneh (right) with President Burns Hargis.

Programs Updates

The programs under the umbrella of the SIS saw growth and expansion. Some experienced needed changes in direction. New leadership also provided the opportunity for evaluation and renewal.

Study Abroad

A brief history of the study abroad program was given in the second part of this book. Much of the material for this section was graciously provided by current director, Jeff Simpson.[3]

The present Study Abroad Office came into being as a result of a FIPSE grant negotiated by the International Programs Office under Art Klatt, with Tim Huff's involvement. The first students were exchanged through that grant in 1995-1996 which necessitated the creation of a formal Study Abroad Office. While housed in several locations across campus over the years, the current Study Abroad Office is located in the newly-renovated Student Union as a way to better connect with students interested in participating in a program abroad. Since relocating to the center of campus, the office has seen a marked increase in student participation. From the first student studying in Japan in 1991, OSU now sends over 700 undergraduate and graduate students abroad each year to earn academic credit applying towards their degrees. The program has seen significant growth in programs led by OSU faculty members as well as an interest in service learning and internship opportunities abroad. OSU holds student exchange agreements with over seventy (70) universities around the world in over thirty (30) different countries. The institution has partnered with eight (8) additional program providers to further expand study and internship opportunities for students and to increase the number of underrepresented students participating in study away programs. OSU students study each year across North and South America, Europe, Asia, Africa and Australia.

The office also administers the National Student Exchange (NSE) program for OSU as an alternative cultural immersion opportunity for students. A member of this 170 institution strong consortium, OSU encourages students to also consider study in other areas of the United States and the U. S. Territories. Several programs in Canada are also included in the NSE consortium. This program is particularly well suited for students in tightly structured degree programs and those who are not yet ready to live abroad for any number of reasons. In 2015 over 30 students either studied away from campus or at OSU through the National Student Exchange.

Assisting students in funding study abroad has always been in the forefront for OSU's international efforts. After the student body failed in their collective efforts to gain state approval for an SGA mandated study abroad fee to help fund study abroad scholarships, then Provost Marlene Strathe stepped in to begin the Provost's Study Abroad Scholarship in 2006. Originally funded with $40,000, the Provost's Study Abroad Scholarship now awards over $175,000 each year to encourage OSU students to participate in study abroad. Another significant shift occurred in the office in 2010 through the generous donation of a $6 million endowment for study abroad scholarship by Donald and Cathey Humphreys as a part of the Branding Success Campaign. Directed at long-term study abroad, the Humphreys' Scholarship sends over twenty (20) students abroad each year and allows students who otherwise would not be able to participate in study abroad to realize their goals and gain academic experience abroad. As well, in 2010 Don and Cathey Humphreys endowed a significant program that generates over $250,000 annually in travel grants administered by 6 Humphreys Faculty Chairs and a long-term program scholarship program administered by the Study Abroad Office. The total funding from OSU sources was nearly $775,000 in 2015.

A direct beneficiary of the Humphreys' Scholarship was Alex Hannah, a junior at OSU. He was able to have an intern experience related to bio-energy production in Brazil at the Univeridade Estadual Paulista in Soa Paulo. He was challenged with speaking and listening in Portuguese. He commented, "It was very humbling, and I learned a lot about the country, and got to see the ocean for first time in my life in Rio de Janeiro while I made new friends, some of which are family to me now. I came home with a different view of the world and of myself."[4]

Evan Black has benefited greatly from study abroad experiences at OSU. A Stillwater native, she studied abroad the summer after her freshman year. Her first experience was through an Arts & Sciences summer language course in Puebla, Mexico, which transformed her academic and professional trajectory. She continued study abroad experiences six times in four countries through the generous gifts and scholarships offered. She graduated from OSU in 2008 with a dual degree in Spanish and Public Relations. She was awarded a Fulbright fellowship in Chile where she served as an English Teaching Assistant at a university. In 2012, Black completed a Rotary International Group Study exchange in Brazil where she focused on issues relating to education and development. Through her continued interest in Latin America and education, she was awarded the Kathryn Davis Fellowship for Peace to study Portuguese at Middlebury College. In May 2013, Black earned her master's degree in Education and Intercultural Communication at the University of Pennsylvania. She now resides in New York City where she focuses on international education, training and career development, consulting with international non-profits.[5]

Matt Clemo was a study abroad student from the University of Hertfordshire who came to study at OSU for a year on exchange. He recounts

"I came to Stillwater during the 2010-2011 academic year because

I'd always wanted to study abroad in another country, and figured I was unlikely to ever just 'visit Oklahoma', so why not live there for a year instead? It turned out to be one of the best decisions I ever made. When I arrived, I received tremendous support helping me to conduct research on the OSU football athletes for my undergraduate research project back in the UK. This opportunity undoubtedly lead me toward a better overall degree classification, and also set me up nicely to pursue further similar research at a postgraduate level. In addition, my experiences at OSU led me to helping other exchange students upon my return to the UK. I began working as a Study Abroad Ambassador for my university to help promote the idea to other students, and I also became the National Representative of an international student organization that helps provide opportunities for cultural understanding to incoming exchange students. Through all of this I got to travel the world, see amazing sights, meet amazing people, and create unforgettable memories. Without a doubt, the experience of studying abroad completely changed my life."[6]

Born in Mexico and raised in Oklahoma, Alejandra Gonzalez learned the importance of cultural appreciation at a young age. While attending Oklahoma State University as a political science and sociology student, Gonzalez studied abroad for a semester in the Czech Republic, an experience that shaped her knowledge of Central Europe and fueled her interest in international travel. Upon return from her semester abroad, Gonzalez began working at her university's study abroad office as a peer advisor, where she was first introduced to the world of international education. Ready to embark on her next academic adventure, Gonzalez enrolled in ISA's summer program in Meknes, Morocco and found herself learning more about the Middle East and North Africa during a fascinating time in world history, the Arab Spring. After graduation, Gonzalez interned with President Obama's campaign in Chicago. She worked to ensure that Latinos could vote in this vital election and helped the Latino Vote team in coordinating a nationwide campaign. She most recently taught English, Model UN, and other subject classes to Spanish middle- and high-school students in Madrid, Spain through a Fulbright grant. Gonzalez is currently working with International Studies Abroad as a program manager for three of the countries she's called home: Czech Republic, Morocco and Spain. Through her experiences, she's been able to blend her interests and skills to find an ideal career in the field of international education. Gonzalez said, "My experiences leading up to and following my first study abroad program have all led me to the field of international education. Study abroad has opened doors for me that I didn't even know existed!",[7]

Gerry Auel, the heart and soul of the study abroad efforts at OSU for over 16 years, retired as director of Study Abroad in July 2012, returning to one of her first loves, the Peace Corps, where she is served a two-year assignment in Burkina Faso. Jeff J. Simpson, former Study Abroad Coordinator in the office, stepped into the role of director to lead the institution's study abroad efforts through rapidly increasing change as more students enter college aiming to study abroad as a part of their degree. Building upon programs developed by previous staff including Marie Noss, Elainor Inglis, Hope Ray, and Heather Cates Brant, Kat (Kratochvilova) Henry and Maggie Jackson the office continues to provide both program and academic advising guided by Aleitha Burgess Stephens, Marissa Hernandez and Josh Pontrelli. Staff members in the office teach two undergraduate courses each year to help prepare students for life in another culture and a reflective journaling course for students to articulate their lived experiences while abroad. A pioneer in student peer advisor development, the office has provided employment to several students each year, many of whom now work within the international education profession at universities, the State Department, and organizations around the U. S. and abroad.

With a primary focus toward increasing the number of students participating in a program abroad, the office is actively developing new and exciting partnerships that better meet the needs of 21st century university students. These include partnerships in diverse locations such as China, Kazakhstan, and Chile, as well as programs more closely aligned with specific degree programs in historically underrepresented disciplines like engineering, nutrition, and education.

Whether participating in long-term or short-term programs, participants agree that the experience broadens their worldview and widens their perspectives both of life in the United States as well as abroad. The Study Abroad/National Student Exchange Office is instrumental in facilitating students' desire to become more independent and to better understand the world in which they live today. In today's climate of global connectedness, the ability to appreciate and interact with individuals from different cultures has become an essential part of an educated citizen.

Graduate Program

In times of unprecedented global change, OSU is providing an educational climate that allows undergraduate students to incorporate international perspectives into their curricula. The International Studies minor became available to all students regardless of their major in the fall of 2011. While the minor is housed in the College of Arts & Sciences, the School of International Studies oversees the minor under the direction of the director of the School of International Studies, Dr. Joel Jenswold. Pia Guymon was the first hired as the undergraduate advisor followed by Janet Herren, a former student in International Studies. She also assumed oversight of the school's affiliated student organizations. She now serves as the undergraduate advisor and the graduate coordinator.

Courses within the minor encourage students to understand social, political, economic and cultural contrasts throughout the world. Students structure their minor from three clusters of courses and learning experiences encompassing International Decision Making (6 credit hours), International Environment (9 credit hours) and International Experience (3 credit hours). In addition, each student must complete 10 credit hours of a foreign language or demonstrate proficiency through examination. International students are exempt from the International Experience but the 3 credit hours must be achieved through other course work on the minor list.

Since its creation as a university-wide minor, 24 students have graduated with the minor, and there are currently 21 undergraduate students from diverse academic disciplines who have officially declared a minor in International Studies. Three students were the first to graduate with an International Studies minor from OSU in May 2012: Kyle Buthod, Alejandra Gonzalez, and Christopher Long. An academic advisor in the School of International Studies works with the undergraduate students to help them declare the minor and select their coursework. The advisor also works with students in Sigma Iota Rho, an honorary student organization for undergraduate and graduate students desiring international studies.

Rafael Zhansultanov, an Edmund S. Muskie Graduate Fellow, along with Pia Guyman and Dr. Joel Jenswold initiated the process for Sigma Iota Rho to have an OSU chapter. Since its inception in 2011, students in Sigma Iota Rho have participated in OSU Homecoming events, hosted documentary screenings about international topics of interest, conducted induction ceremonies for new students, and participated in International Day at the Capital. Beyond this, members have worked to recruit new members and advertise their new organization.

Some students who receive the minor continue their education in this field in our International Studies master's program. Dawson Metcalf, a 2013 OSU Outstanding Senior and 2011 Freeman Indonesia Nonprofit Intern, is an example of a remarkable undergraduate student who is continuing his education. One of his goals in the graduate program is to serve in the Peace Corps. Dawson says he has, "chosen to pursue the Peace Corps because we are all citizens of this planet, and we're meant to help one another. I firmly believe, people are responsible for the social problems that we see all over the globe, and people have to challenge those issues if we have any hope of creating a better future." Dawson served as President of Sigma Iota Rho and Vice President of External Affairs for the Student Association for Global Affairs.[9]

In 2010-2011 the graduate program curriculum was reformed. Major changes included the transformation of the only universally required course (Global Issues) and the addition of required coursework in research design.

New course designations for independent study and study abroad were added. One result of this was the ability to offer program credit for a certification course as an international business professional in cooperation with the Trade and Development Center.

Beginning in 2011, graduate assistants from the International Studies Masters' program were assigned to individual faculty members around the university as research assistants. This provided a significant scholarly opportunity for students. It also built goodwill with the various colleges and departments as more of their own assistantship resources were freed up and more faculty members were provided with research assistance.

Benefactors Don and Cathey Humphreys established endowed faculty chairs in International Studies with a mandate to support long-term student activities abroad. The first three Humphreys Chairs were Dr. Shida Henneberry (Agricultural Economics), Dr. Joel Jenswold (Political Science and International Studies), and Dr. Kevin Voss (Marketing). Current Chairs include Dr. Reuel Hanks (Geography), Dr. Shida Henneberry, Dr. Paulette Hebert (Design, Housing and Merchandising), Dr. Joel Jenswold, and Dr. Kevin Voss. The application process for interested students was instituted in Fall 2013. The endowment program is structured to provide for a total of six chairs over the ensuing few years.

Changes in university policy in 2012 resulted in much more attractive terms for prospective graduate assistants. At the same time, the number of such assistantships was correspondingly reduced.

Since 2010 the Academic Programs Office has adopted a higher profile in supporting visiting scholars. In addition to coordinating the Junior Faculty Development Program of the U.S. State Department, the office offers support functions such as library access, office support, and admission to campus recreational facilities for visiting foreign scholars in any of the university academic programs.

[The author acknowledges the work of Joel Jenswold and Janet Herren in providing the information above in this department.[10] He also provided updated materials for the list of SIS graduate students and data in the Appendix.]

English Language Institute

[The author acknowledges the contributions of Kay Keys in providing the information in this section below.]

Facts and Figures

In the five-year time period from Spring 2009 through Fall 2013, the English Language Institute (ELI) has continued to carry out its mission of helping non-native students achieve the level of English proficiency required to enter and succeed in a U.S. institution of higher education. Students range from 18-year-old high school graduates venturing abroad to earn a bachelor's degree to 50-year-old mid-career professionals seeking master's or doctoral degrees. Some are family sponsored, but a large number have been awarded scholarships by their governments or their places of employment, principally universities. Annual enrollment figures for ELI have increased gradually over this five-year time period from 178 to a Fall 2013 enrollment of 296, maximum capacity for space currently allocated to the Institute. Enrollment lists during this same period include students from the following 43 countries (all continents except Antarctica and Australia):

Angola	Macedonia
Benin	Malaysia
Brazil	Mali
Burkina Faso	Mexico
China	Moldova
Colombia	Nepal
Congo	Oman
Czech Republic	Paraguay
Ecuador	Peru
Ethiopia	Qatar
Honduras	Romania
Hungary	Saudi Arabia
India	Spain
Indonesia	Sweden
Iran	Taiwan
Iraq	Thailand
Japan	Turkey
Jordan	UAE
Korea	United States*
Kuwait	Venezuela
Libya	Vietnam
Lithuania	

*These individuals hold U.S. citizenship because they were born in the U.S. They do not have proficiency in English, however, because they were raised in another country.

While the Institute is governed by OSU and its faculty and staff members are OSU employees, the Institute continues to operate solely on funds generated by the tuition and fees paid by its students. From its inception in 1970, no state monies have ever been allocated for the operation of the Institute. Faculty and staff salaries, equipment, materials, and all operational costs are earned by the unit.

Special Contract Programs

In addition to providing between 132 and 154 classes per week in the regular sixteen-week fall and spring semesters and the eight-week summer session, the English Language Institute frequently designs special programs to meet the needs of groups, usually sponsored by a university or government agency. One such program, begun in 2002, continues, with students from Kansai Gaidai University (KGU) participating in an English-only Study Abroad program. While ELI assigns grades for the semester or academic year, the home university, KGU, awards the credit. In another continuing program, implemented in 2010, Tecnológico de Monterrey has contracted with ELI to provide four-week language training courses for professors, administrators, and students from a number of their Mexican campuses. These programs have been carried out in cooperation with IS&O, whose staff has scheduled cultural activities for the groups during their stays. In 2011, ELI provided a three-week language program for 36 Chinese students, many of whom were honors students, from Southwest Jiaotong University (SWJTU). This program was offered in conjunction with the OSU College of Engineering and the ISS Office as a part of SWJTU□s first study abroad □Engineering Excellence□ project. In Fall 2012 and Fall 2013, the International Research and Exchanges Board (IREX) sent small groups of students from Basra University in Iraq for six-week language training programs. Thai Nguyen University of Technology (TNUT) contracted for a group of administrators to improve their language skills during the summer of 2012. ELI expects to provide a similar program for this Vietnamese university again in 2013 and is currently in the very early states of developing projects with a Brazilian university.

Reviews

In 2012 and 2013, the English Language Institute successfully underwent two regular external reviews and an internal financial audit, receiving continued approval from each reviewing entity. Evaluators chosen by the Oklahoma State Regents for Higher Education awarded the maximum five-year approval following their evaluation of the ELI Self-Study and their subsequent on-site visit. Also, the University and College Intensive English Programs (UCIEP) Consortium gave full approval for continued membership in the prestigious organization following their regular review of extensive documentation and a follow-up site visit. Both of these reviews entailed an in-depth study of every aspect of the Institute, to include the mission, curriculum, textbook selection, administrator and faculty qualifications, professional development opportunities, student and faculty evaluation, testing, recordkeeping, finances, use of technology, and physical facilities. In addition to these external academic reviews, ELI successfully completed an internal financial audit conducted by OSU Board of Regents Internal Audits.

Plans for the Future

After 44 years with OSU, 25 of which she served as director of ELI, Kay Woodruff Keys retired at the end of 2013. After a national search for her successor, Dr. Deborah Osborne assumed leadership responsibilities for the Institute in January 2014 – January 2016. Fred Griffiths took over leadership in January 2016.

The above reviews have clearly demonstrated that the Institute is academically, operationally, and financially sound and poised for continued development. The groundwork has been laid for technological upgrades, possible expansion, and movement toward CEA accreditation.[11]

An ELI ice cream social.

ELI students at Pikes Peak.

Fulbright Program

An important national program continuing its activity on the OSU campus through the School of International Studies is the Fulbright Program. Directed by Steven Hallgren, this is a highly competitive program designed to assist individuals for international studies and experiences through grants, scholarships and fellowships.

The Fulbright Program is the U.S. Government's flagship academic exchange effort for students, professionals, artists and scholars. It was started in 1946 by the efforts of Senator J. William Fulbright and is conducted through the United States Department of State, Bureau of Educational and Cultural Affairs. The Fulbright Program offers a variety of grant opportunities, including comprehensive grants for 6 to 12 months and travel grants. There are opportunities in over 140 countries for research, study and teaching. The program includes bilateral agreements for exchanges in both directions with each host country.

Oklahoma State University has a long history of participation

Fulbright Programs by students, faculty members and administrators. There are nearly 100 persons at OSU who have participated in a Fulbright program or are currently a grantee. We have numerous faculty members and administrators who have traveled abroad on a Fulbright program. Each year 15 to 25 Fulbright students and scholars from an equal number of countries study, teach and research at OSU. In addition, each year three to five of our students receive awards from the Fulbright US Student Program to research, study or teach in a foreign country.

Many OSU students have benefited from the opportunity to learn and explore in an international, academic experience. For the 2012-2013 academic year, eight OSU students received Fulbright Awards. Tyler Van Arsdale, an entrepreneurship student, was awarded an English Teaching Assistantship in South Korea. Caitlin Cleary was awarded an English Teaching Assistantship to Turkey. Joshua Damron conducted physical science research in Germany. Alejandra Gonzalez Herrera taught English to secondary school students in Spain. Jesi Lay, a biosystems and agricultural engineering student, was awarded to study engineering in Sirra Leone. Erin Nordquist was awarded by the French Ministry of Education a teaching position in Montpellier, France. Latasha Wilson, a political science and German major was awarded an English Teaching Assistantship to Turkey. Meredith Wyatt also taught as an English Teaching Assistant in Bogota, Columbia.[13]

The Center also offers over 15 information sessions over the course of the year to both students and faculty to bring great awareness of the opportunities available to those populations through Fulbright Programs. These efforts have resulted in increasing numbers of scholarships and grants being awarded to OSU students and faculty. Since Dr. Steve Hallgren took over as the Fulbright advisor in 2006, OSU has produced ninety-seven applications for national review, of which twenty-one were awarded Fulbright Fellowships.

Fulbright students at a cookout.

Peace Corps

Peace Corps recruiting continues on an active basis at OSU. In its fifty-year national history, hundreds of thousands of people have sacrificially represented the United States in helping others around the world. As a part of the School of International Studies, participation in the Peace Corps can also be part of a master's degree program. Many OSU students have gained personal benefit from helping others in international settings. An SIS grad, Billy Worthy, served in La Aldea, Costa Rica for two years. He worked with children, adults and youth on a variety of projects from building a park of recycled materials to teaching English on and doing workshops on HIV/AIDS awareness. Diana Gardner, another SIS grad, served in Namibia for two years. She worked mostly with women and teenagers in Okhandja in the prevention of mother to child transmission of HIV/AIDS. She also taught children in math, English, life skills, Bible study, reading, art and sports.[14]

Phi Beta Delta and Sigma Iota Rho

Two honor societies are active on the OSU campus. Phi Beta Delta is the first honor society to promote international understanding and to recognize individuals who have demonstrated scholarly achievement in international education and exchange.

In December 2003, sixteen years after the establishment of the national society, Oklahoma State University's Epsilon Upsilon chapter was granted membership by the national board of directors. Sixty students, faculty and staff were inducted as new members at the chapter's induction ceremony on April 7, 2004. Today, the chapter numbers over 250 members, 34 of whom are honorary.

Based in part on a strong student scholarship program to help students present their research at international conferences and the mentorship of new, international chapters within the national organization, the Epsilon Upsilon Chapter received the Outstanding Chapter Award for the Southwest Region in 2012.[15]

Sigma Iota Rho honors the scholastic achievements and dedication to international studies. It was established at OSU in the spring of 2011.

Mexico Liaison Offices

Instituto Tecnológico y de Estudios Superiores de Monterrey (ITESM)

ITESM is one of the leading universities in Latin America. It is a private, non-partisan and secular university founded in 1943 by a group of visionary Mexicans led by Eugenio Garza Sada. It has developed into 33 campuses distributed all over Mexico including everything from high school to doctoral studies and a Virtual University which provides it with an international platform. Part of ITESM's mission is to form professionals with integrity, ethical standards and a humanistic outlook, who are internationally competitive in their professional field. These characteristics found in OSU a strategic partner and in 2005 a Contractual Agreement for Reciprocal Student Exchange program between ITESM-Chihuahua Campus and OSU was signed.

In 2007, thanks to the Mexico-liaison office and the leadership at the Chihuahua Campus with then director, Joaquin Guerra, OSU hosted for the first time a group of 21 undergraduate engineering and business students from Chihuahua for a four-week summer program. Students were able to further their academic education at OSU as well as experience a different language and culture. They were immersed in the university's student life and on the weekends were able to experience surrounding cities, museums and cultural venues that introduced them to Oklahoma history.

Luis Serrano, from ITESM-Chihuahua Campus, is a success story that developed from the beginning of this institutional collaboration. He was one of the participants of the exchange program at OSU in 2008, thanks to the great experience he had and the welcoming environment for which OSU is known. He decided to come back to pursue a master's degree in the Biosystems & Agricultural Engineering department where he was hired as a graduate assistant and in 2010 became one of 10 winners in OSU's $1 billion fundraising campaign, Branding Success.

Despite the external impacts of 2009, mentioned before when summer programs with Mexico were suspended, the relationship between OSU and ITESM- Chihuahua Campus continued to grow. During the spring and fall semesters of 2009-2010, faculty collaboration was pursued through the International Visiting Scholars program. This program was meant to foster greater interest in academic collaboration at the international level and stimulate cross-cultural interactions and understanding between Mexico and the United States as well as encourage collaboration on teaching, research and extension programs in a variety of academic topics. Consequently, faculty from the Oklahoma State University visited various ITESM campuses in Northern Mexico. As guest speakers, the professors gave lectures supplementary to content that students are learning about in core courses.

In the fall of 2009, Dr. Ning Wang, Associate professor of Mechatronics at OSU visited Chihuahua, where she lectured about various Mechatronic topics and discussed with students their course projects and other Electronic Technology projects. Dr. Wang was very pleased with this experience and commented that: "The teaching facility in the department and college of engineering is very advanced. I was very impressed. I enjoyed meeting faculty members from other countries: When I was in the university, two professors from Peru and Argentina were there also. I was very pleased to meet and discuss with them. I enjoyed the trip to Chihuahua. It changed my view of Mexican universities, students, and culture quite a lot. I also enjoy working with the professors in the university."[16]

This initial contact allowed continued collaboration among faculty. For example, Dr. Camilo Lozoya form ITESM-Chihuahua Campus was awarded a substantial grant from Mexico's National Council of Science and Technology (CONACYT) and in summer of 2013 came to OSU to discuss with Dr. Wang about collaborating in this research project funded by CONACYT. He is also interested in sending a group of students in the summer to explore other research projects.

Administrators and academic leaders from both ITESM and OSU envisioned furthering their collaboration and in 2010, with great effort from Mexico liaison office and Claudia Gutiérrez, director of international programs for the Chihuahua Campus, the ITESM-OSU liaison office was inaugurated. ITESM- Chihuahua Campus sent Verenise Calzadillas and Brisia Hermosillo to lead the office at the Wes Watkins Center, hoping to bridge both institutions' missions to pursue and support academic, cultural, and business exchanges among Mexico, OSU and Oklahoma.

As part of the inauguration ceremony program, the Allegro performed for the first time at the Seretean Concert Hall. Allegro is a student organization that has 25 years of tradition at the ITESM-Chihuahua Campus. It is a spectacular show that brings together high school and undergraduate students to present concerts that include various genres. As an example of the cultural exchange the institutional collaboration encourages, OSU has welcomed Allegro every year since to perform at the Seretean Contert Hall, where students and the community have the opportunity to enjoy various music styles in Spanish and English. The audience expressed their surprise when they found out that these talented musicians, singers and dancers were regular engineer, business or medicine students, with no music related majors.

From 2010 to 2012 Verenise Calzadillas and Brisia Hermosillo welcomed ITESM students and faculty members to participate in the summer programs they prepared for them. Upon completion

Allegro performing on the OSU campus.

Allegro performing on the OSU campus.

of the master degrees they pursued at OSU, Brisia Hermosillo went back to Chihuahua to continue collaborating with the ITESM-Chihuahua Campus Dean of Engineering as a student advisor for the Mechanical Engineering major and Verenise Calzadillas went on to work for Engonex, an Energy company in Oklahoma City.

Marissa Hernandez came to OSU during the summer of 2012 to replace Calzadillas and Hermosillo as well as at the same time pursue her degree in the International Studies Master's program. She led this program from 2012- 2015 and upon finishing her degree in SIS moved across campus to the Study Abroad office where she currently serves as an academic advisor.

In January of 2013 ITESM-OSU liaison offered the first One-on-One Program for university administrators and welcomed the Continued Education Rector for ITESM's Northern Zone, Pedro Facio, to participate in this week-long English immersion program. In addition to practicing the language, he met with OSU's leadership and discussed further collaboration projects. He also enjoyed university and professional basketball games.

Along with the summer faculty led, faculty development, leadership and other academic programs the liaison office has hosted ITESM's coaches who wished to participate in OSU's football clinics. Here coaches had a chance to meet their peers from other universities and learn from each other, benefiting ITESM's Rams (school mascot).

The ITESM-OSU liaison office also encourages OSU students to participate in exchange programs at any of the ITESM campuses in Mexico. Students are welcome to participate in summer academic or internship programs, as well as semester or yearlong exchange programs.

As of July 2013, Joaquin Guerra moved to Monterrey, Mexico to become the Rector for Internationalization of ITESM's system. This marked a new era and further ITESM-OSU collaboration efforts. New winter programs, short and long term academic exchange, dual degree programs and various other projects took place due to Guerra's new position and OSU's relationship with ITESM and Mexico continues to strengthen.

IS&O leads a spring break study abroad course in Chihuahua, Mexico. Beginning with an inaugural class of fifteen participants in 2015, students from all over OSU now have the chance to visit the

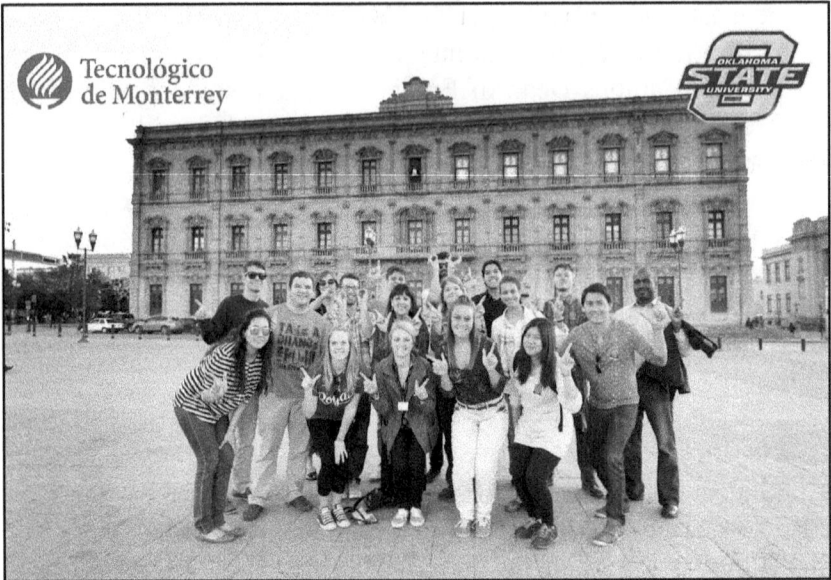

OSU students visit Mexico.

largest state in Mexico, attend classes at one of that country's most prestigious institutions, explore state-of-the-art agricultural and food production facilities, high-tech factories, and economically significant tourism areas; all while earning academic credit. This affordable study abroad opportunity is possible because of the generous support of ITESM and Higher Education.

[The author is also indebted to Marissa Hernandez for providing the above information.[17]]

International Outreach

Outreach Unit

The International Outreach Unit promotes international research, education and development on behalf of OSU and the state of Oklahoma through building worldwide linkages; pursuing and coordinating collaborative projects; and reaching out to state, national and international audiences. It serves to provide high-quality, academic, short-term programs for internationals in order to achieve and maintain a global mindset in participants. The Outreach Unit provides the on and off-campus logistical arrangements, academic presentations, cultural/academics visits and entertainment activities for international individuals.

There are three core programs: Experience Oklahoma, High School Summer Academy and Faculty-Led short international academic and multicultural experiences. Directing the program is Rodrigo Tello.

A native of Mexico, Tello attended the UPAEP and graduated in 2007 with a degree in Hotel and Restaurant Management. He became acquainted with the dual degree program with OSU. He began his dual degree work toward a master's degree at UPAEP in 2009. In January 2011 Tello moved to Stillwater to continue his dual degree studies. That summer he was invited to work as an intern supporting the summer programs between UPAEP and OSU. He hosted a delegation of over forty students. After graduation, he received approval for temporary immigrant work status. He was offered and accepted the directorship position of the Outreach Unit August 2012. He made recruitment trips to Mexico and has seen the number of participants in the summer programs increase each year.[18]

The summer programs' growth has been steady since Tello started. In 2012 there were 303 summer participants, 316 participants in 2013 and 539 participated in the summer of 2014.

Experience Oklahoma

Correspondence Education

To meet the wartime need for sugar in 1921, President James B. Eskridge established a correspondence school at Oklahoma A & M College, beginning with a beekeeping course. Though a seeming unorthodox offering, Correspondence Education (CE) has endured over the past 95 years through this same flexibility.

From paper/pencil booklets; to "study centers" whereby instructors met with six plus students a week at common locations away from campus; to the 60 mixed online, CD/DVD, and print media Oklahoma State University (OSU) credit courses offered today, CE has continued to fulfill our mission of reaching more learners and providing those learners accessibility to quality Oklahoma State University education.

Also toward that goal, in a collaboration with the OSU International Students and Scholars Office, CE previously facilitated undergraduate honors engineering students from Southwest Jiaotong University of Chengdu, China, to complete Engineering 2213 (Thermodynamics). This course is a standard part of any second-year engineering undergraduate curriculum. It is also a component of China's national "Engineering Excellence" Project that strives to enhance engineering education through international curriculum collaboration.

CE has been affiliated with The Center for Legal Studies (CLS) for several years now. CLS is one of America's most respected legal education training centers, offering 11 non-credit legal programs nationally since 1980. Certificates of completion are issued through and bear the OSU logo. These courses are especially popular with military personnel/spouses and incarcerated persons.

Another component of the OSU CE program is a partnership with Condensed Curriculum International (CCI) to offer 10 Health Ed Today online non-credit e-learning medical courses. CCI is a leading education organization also including Pearson Education and E-College. Under consideration at this time is the addition of their new Business & Management, IT, Software & Web Development, Healthcare, Green Technology, Project Management, Academic Foundations, and Workforce Readiness courses.

It continues its relevance in meeting student needs through wonderful testimonies. Taylor England took CE courses because of her ability to work 30 hours a week while continuing studies in her major area. She commented, "Also the professors gave great feedback, and really helped express their opinions on the assignments." Julie Rose had similar experiences with her CE courses. She stated, "Sometimes life doesn't allow for a prospective student to sit in a classroom and learn. These classes are very beneficial to parents of children or someone with a fulltime job who is trying to further their education."

Thus, from its beginning versatility has been an earmark of the Oklahoma State University Correspondence Education department. CE will continue to move forward to provide independent study opportunities to learners whose work, family responsibilities, physical isolation or medical concerns may preclude participation in regularly-scheduled class meetings.[19]

Memorandum of Understanding

With the complexities of establishing cooperative agreements with international educational institutions and facilities, a Memorandum of Understanding is a necessary tool for initiating the detailed process. After these general agreements are reached, a more detailed Activity Agreement is created by the Dean of the OSU college involved and the cooperating institution. To date, OSU, through Jim Shideler, has agreements with 370 educational institutions in 94 countries. The countries and institutions are Argentina (1), Armenia (1), Australia (3), Austria (1), Azerbaijan (1), Belgium (3), Belize (1), Botswana (2), Brazil (4), Cameroon (1), Canada (3), China (23), Costa Rica (5), Czech Republic (2), Democratic Republic of the Congo (1), Denmark (1), England (7), Estonia (1), Ethiopia (10), Finland (1), France (8), Germany (6), Ghana (1), Honduras (1), Iceland (1), India (22), Indonesia (4), Ireland (3), Italy (7), Jamaica (1), Japan (4), Jordan (2), Kazakhstan (3), Kenya (2), Lithuania (1), Malawi (1), Malaysia (4), Mali (2), Malta (1), Mexico (14), Moldova (1), Mongolia (2), Mozambique (4), Netherlands (4), Nigeria (1), Norway (1), Oman (1), Pakistan (1), Peru (2), Philippines (1), Portugal (1), Puerto Rico (1), Romania (1), Russia (4), Saudi Arabia (1), Scotland (1), Sierra Leone (1), Slovakia (1), Slovenia (1), South Africa (1), South Korea (9), Spain (4), Sweden (2), Switzerland (1), Taiwan (2), Thailand (10), Tunisia

(1), Turkey (4), Ukraine (1), United Arab Emirates (2), United States of America (2), Venezuela (1), Viet Nam (3) and Zambia (2).[20]

Center for International Trade and Development

Although not directly under the title of the School of International Studies, the newly-revitalized Center for International Trade and Development incorporates various aspects of the international studies experiences. The following information was provided by Anthony Cambas.

Background

The CITD can be traced back to the late 1980s and early 1990s and the tireless efforts of former Congressman Wes Watkins. In addition to the importance of providing resources and technical assistance to help Oklahoma-based companies expand their exports, Congressman Watkins believed that it was imperative to expand international development activities.

Background History of the Center for International Trade and Development

The Center for International Trade and Development is one of the units of the Division of International Studies and Outreach and its core activities rest on two pillars: international trade and international development. Although in the past there have been different centers at OSU dealing with international trade, the genesis of the CITD as it functions today goes back to January 2010 when Professor Mike Dicks was named the Wes and Lou Watkins Chair for International Trade and Development, a position that he held through December 2012.

During the time that Dr. Dicks occupied the chair position, he oversaw the efforts and set the foundations for the CITD to receive funding. He established a working framework and foundation for an international trade center that would provide high-quality export assistance to Oklahoma-based small and medium sized companies. Dr. Dicks began the process to search for staff.

CITD Staff

By the end of 2011, two International Trade Specialists Anthony Cambas and Justin Hazzard were hired to help build the CITD's foundation and to get the center up and running in the areas of international trade assistance and in international development. In the fall of 2012, Kate Arroyo who was working as Grad Assistant and who was a graduate of the OSU Masters in International Studies with a specialization in International Trade and Development was hired as an International Trade Specialist. Arroyo worked with the CITD through September 2013 when she took a job as an International Trade Specialist with the University of North Florida in Jacksonville, Florida. Although no longer with the CITD, Arroyo played an important role with the center in its formative stage and will always be remembered for her role. Justin Hazzard has also left CITD and took a position with Meridian Technology Center as the Director of Center for Business Development.

As of December 2015, the CITD staff is comprised of Director, Anthony Cambas; International Trade Specialist, Assoumane Maiga; and Financial Coordinator, Rebekah Kidanemariam. The CITD staff fits well into IS&O because they speak several languages, and have extensive international experience in the academic, business, technical assistance and international development areas.[21]

One of the interesting connections with the SIS, Ethiopia and the CITD is Rebekah Kidanemariam. She is currently the Financial Coordinator of CITD and International Trade Center -SBDC. She holds a Master of Science degree in International Studies, focusing on Business and Economics, from the School of International Studies at Oklahoma State University (OSU). She also has a Bachelor of Art Degree in Accounting from Haramaya University in Ethiopia. Kidanemariam's presence with the CITD staff helps uphold the long and proud tradition that Oklahoma State University has with Ethiopia dating back to the times of former OSU President Henry Bennett in the 1950s as Haramaya University was established with the help of OSU in 1954 making it one of the renowned universities in the country and among one of the country's earliest establishments.[22]

The Wes Watkins Distinguished Lectureships continued with past speakers including Dr. Condoleezza Rice, Jim Clifton and Paul Weisenfeld.

Tony Cambas, Director, International Trade and Development in Brazil.

Recent International Impact

The period from 2009 until the present saw the impact on international study at OSU. Major U. S. war on terrorism involvement escalated and de-escalated in Iraq and Afghanistan. Destructive natural disasters- domestic and international- brought nations together for relief efforts. Economic crises continued to hamper development and created unrest in many countries. Increasing improvements and availability of personal communication devises helped to provide immediate awareness of national crises. With all of these experiences, new doors were opened and new opportunities for expansion were offered for OSU's School of International Studies.

Future Dreams

As universities are careful to always consider the future in their planning and operations, so it is with the SIS. Some of the needs discovered after the tenth anniversary were met. Others have gone unaddressed. It is hoped that the number of students involved in international studies through OSU will increase. It is also hoped that the number of students graduating from the SIS will go on to pursue further post-graduate degrees. As the number of OSU grads with international experiences are stationed throughout the world, a growing number of influential contacts will be established for potential Oklahoma business development. Those contacts may also recruit future international students for OSU and the SIS. More OSU alums and other visionaries will see the importance of major gifts to OSU for increased involvement in international study experiences.

The International Strategic plan was finalized in 2015 and spells out the hopes for Oklahoma State University's future international endeavors.

International Strategic plan top priorities:

1. Study Abroad, International Service Learning and International Internships
   a. Increaseparticipationineducationabroadprogramsto50percentofundergraduatestudents,measuredrelativetothenumber of yearly graduating seniors in each academic college.

2. International Students and Scholars
Increase undergraduate student recruiting by participating annually in study abroad fairs, with central coordination facilitating participation from the colleges 2,200 International Students would be the highest enrollment in the past 30 years.

3. Strategic International Partnerships
Enhance and Maintain University level strategic international partnerships in China, Mexico and Ethiopia and support additional college level strategic partners in countries appropriate for the international activities of those colleges.

4.   Serve the International Needs of the State of Oklahoma

Contribute to the economic development of Oklahoma through a planned effort to enhance the internationalization and export capacity of businesses in Oklahoma.

5.   Develop an administrative structure at OSU that engages the University and broader community in all international issues affecting Oklahoma State University.

Reformulate the International Advisory Council to consist of representatives from each College and selected administrative units.
   a.   Create an International Advocacy Council which meets annually to become better informed about internationalization efforts at Oklahoma State University and which supports the international efforts of the University.

6.   Enhance Foreign Language and Global/Cultural Scholarship.

7.   Expand and Achieve Excellence in English as a Second Language Instruction.

Increase enrollment in the English Language Institute by 50 percent while enhancing the number of ELI students who enroll at OSU and are successful in their programs.

8.   Affirm the Need to Recognize, Support and Reward the International Activities of OSU Employees.

Support international travel of OSU employees by registering the travel with the Department of State, applying for international travel insurance, providing them information on OSU's Memorandums of Understanding in their destination countries and the opportunity to network with other OSU faculty who have recently travelled to the same destination.

   a.   Encourage Department Heads to request information on international activities and scholarship for annual appraisals.

9.   Engage with Prospective Donors and Create Awareness of Opportunities to Support Internationalization at Oklahoma State University.

10. Increase the International Capacity of OSU Employees.

Provide foreign language training for current employees

a.   Offer training programs on study abroad programs, Fulbright programs, international trade development, strategic partnerships and agreements, international academic programs, and other topics where education could improves OSU's human capital in the international arena.

The base of *legacy*, the past and present *leadership*, and the ongoing process of *learning* all give a positive picture *looking into the future* of the international studies experiences at Oklahoma State University.

Conclusion

In considering the leadership and learning of the Oklahoma State University School of International Studies, the question has come to mind, "What would Henry Bennett think of the School of International Studies?" Having posed that question to many in personal interviews, several answers can be given. First, Bennett would be awed by the strong academic emphasis and proud of the achieved status of the university. As an educator and believer in accredited programs and degrees, he would be very pleased with the academic direction and status of the international studies program today. At first glance Bennett might be disappointed in the apparent lack of "hands-on" international activities by the university in providing direct technical assistance to the developing countries of the world today. But there are many changes from Bennett's first venture of the college's participation through the Point Four program. There are certainly more political and departmental levels that must dealt with than Bennett had. With the creation of the State Department's United States Agency for International Development as a continuation of Point Four, Bennett would be pleased with the organization and purpose, but he might be disappointed at the lack of funding and national support for such efforts today. As director of the Point Four program, Bennett certainly had more political and fund-raising clout. There is also more competition as an increasing number of colleges and universities compete in recruiting international students and for contract funding for international ventures.

Bennett would appreciate the effort to combine the many internal programs at OSU under the umbrella of the School of International Studies. It would be along the lines of his original plans for the Office of International Programs. Bennett would be excited by the creation of the Peace Corps program and its active presence on campus. Under the umbrella of the School of International Studies, it does offer the hands-on international activity of which Bennett would have been familiar. It also has the unique program at

OSU that allows Peace Corps participation to be a part of a master's degree program in international studies. The continuation of the Study Abroad program would certainly meet with his approval.

What makes the SIS work? It is that combination of understanding and appreciating the *legacy* of the university's history, recognition for continued quality leadership, a constant awareness of the mutual learning and planning for the future. The life and contributions of Henry Bennett must never be forgotten. The recognition of the contributions made by those early brave volunteers of Oklahoma A & M faculty and staff who ventured into foreign lands, even with their families, for long-term assignments must be honored. The dedicated contributions of faculty and staff who cooperated in establishing the School of International Studies must remain as a reminder of what is needed to continue the program.

What will make the SIS continue to work is committed *leadership* in the administration and faculty. The university must have a president who will provide the leadership for campus-wide communication of the purpose and programs of the SIS. The SIS will need a strong leader with academic credibility, university cooperation and a world vision. The university colleges must provide leaders who appreciate and cooperate with efforts to involve their students in participation of international activities. It is imperative that the committed faculty continues to offer their services in the cooperative efforts of the SIS Graduate Program. Their classroom instruction and personal advising are contributions that are necessary and long lasting.

An important requirement for making the SIS work is the ability to appreciate the benefits of mutual *learning* experiences. Evaluations are needed to correct problems and improve the elements of the program that are mutually beneficial. As international experiences continue, awareness must be considered of the significant changes and adjustments that occur. There must be openness to the lessons we can learn from other cultures that may benefit the SIS programs.

An ability to *look into the future* is essential in maintaining and improving the program's sustainability in an ever-changing world. An ongoing documentation of the SIS history must continue to provide the lessons learned from the past to ensure stability for the SIS in the future.

A native of Tulsa, Robert Garrett, came to OSU because of

his family's many OSU connections. Garrett came to OSU with an experience in the Army following high school. After his bachelor's degree, Garrett spent a year studying abroad in the United Kingdom. From there he moved to Asia, teaching English in Korea for one year and in Thailand for two years. Garrett wanted to continue his education toward a master's degree in teaching English as a second language. The SIS was found to be the perfect place to accomplish his academic goals. He received his degree in Marketing and Business in December 2006. Garrett stated that in the SIS he "learned how to be a professional." He recalled, "There were many 'learning' experiences that took place outside of the classroom that I don't think would've been available or offered by other programs. I was constantly exposed to situations where I could interact with business and academic professionals." After SIS, Garrett was employed by a U. S. company to set up sales and manufacturing operations in China. He then pursued a Ph. D in Geography at OSU. In considering his future, Garrett stated "I'm completely dedicated in maintaining a focus on global or international affairs... and continue to build upon the lessons and knowledge I gained from SIS."[1]

After all of the research, interviews and collection of student stories, there has been one central thought that rises to the surface-- *Never underestimate the power and influence of a life motivated and equipped for the service of others.* Reflecting on Henry Bennett, James Halligan, James Hromas, David Hennberry and Burns Hargis, it is encouraging to think of the potential and possibilities for others to rise to the level of leadership that can have a positive international influence. With many students graduating from the SIS in service to the world, there is hope and the possibility for a better world and improvement of lives around the world.

Acknowledgments

Many people are deserving of recognition for the contributions that they have made to this work. Most important are the staff of the School of International Studies and in particular the office of the International Education and Outreach program. The initial prime mover and organizer of all good things was Nikkie Dunnigan. She had assembled scattered files and materials into one office and organized them into a dozen four-drawer filing cabinets. The advantages of such a research room was immeasurable and will be significant for future researchers. Assisting Nikkie was a graduate of the OSU School of International Studies, Svetlana Vasileva. Svetlana came from Bulgaria on a track scholarship. She completed her undergraduate degree in journalism and her master's degree in the SIS. She was assigned to assist me in research and in addition was able to provide proofreading for the early manuscript. Jim Shideler continued his role as gracious coordinator of interviews, provider of requested resources and doing everything to make my many visits to the campus enjoyable and productive. The initial office support staff of Christina Roberts, Liz (Howard) Domnick, Karen Bowers and Danny Darnell were always available to provide research support, encouragement and friendship. Then director James Hromas gave his time and candid observations that were helpful and important in giving historical credibility to this work.

The current staff of the International Studies Office have continued the tradition of gracious assistance and wonderful hospitality. Cathie Kincaid, Karen Bowers, Katie (Reim) Sewell and Jim Shideler have been very supportive and encouraging throughout this project. They were very helpful in proofreading and editing assistance. Katie was helpful in providing access to articles in the great International Studies and Outreach monthly newsletters she produces. Dr. Henneberry has been a very helpful guiding and authoritative voice in completing this project. He also has been gracious with his time and personal encouragement.

Many faculty and staff members of Oklahoma State University

were gracious in providing time for interviews and sharing personal perspectives. Many of these were directly involved in the creation of the School of International Studies. Those with emeriti status were very important with their institutional knowledge. President Burns Hargis was especially kind in working this author into his busy schedule and especially in writing the Foreword to this book.

My wife, Jan, provided important proofreading assistance. David and Gaytha Suits, longtime friends, also provided proofreading assistance. Also providing great assistance in proofreading and editing was Deborah Root. She is a graduate of the OSU doctoral program in journalism and works on the faculty of Ouachita Baptist University in Arkadelphia, Arkansas (The school where Henry Bennett graduated in 1907.).

I am especially indebted to General Doug Dollar, publisher at the New Forums Press in Stillwater, Oklahoma. He has been gracious in publishing my seven earlier works. He is an alum of OSU and an admirer of Henry Bennett's life and accomplishments. Doug is also a retired major general still very active in the Army Reserves. Doug and his wife, Gayla, have offered encouragement in the projects, expertise in the details of publishing and great friendship with myself and all at OSU involved in this project.

Appendix

Presidents and Acting Presidents

Oklahoma State University

1.	1891 – 1894	R. J. Barker	(1st President)
2.	1894 – 1895	Henry E. Alvord	(2nd President)
3.	1-6/1895	Edmund D. Murdaugh	(3rd President)
4.	1895 – 1899	George E. Morrow	(4th President)
5.	1899 – 1908	Angelo C. Scott	(5th President)
6.	1908 – 1914	James Henry Connell	(6th President)
7.	1914 – 1915	Lowry L. Lewis	(7th President)
8.	1915 – 1921	James W. Cantwell	(8th President)
9.	1921 – 1923	James E. Eskridge	(9th President)
10.	6-7/1923	George E. Wilson	*(acting president)*
11.	8-9/1923	Richard Gaines Tyler	*(acting president)*
12.	1923 – 1928	Bradford Knapp	(10th President)
13.	5-6/1928	Clarence H. McElroy	*(acting president)*
14.	1928 – 1951	Henry Garland Bennett	(11th President)
15.	1952 – 1966	Oliver S. Willham	(12th President)
16.	1966 – 1977	Robert Kamm	(13th President)
17.	1977 -1988	Lawrence Boger	(14th President)
18	1988 – 1993	John R. Campbell	(15th President)
19.	1994 - 2003	James E. Halligan	(16th President
20.	2003 – 2007	David J. Schmidly	(17th President)
21.	2008 -present	V. Burns Hargis	(18th President)

Henry G. Bennett, Administrator of the Point Four Program

(Speech at Rome, Italy, November 19, 1951 at the Sixth Session of the United Nations Food and Agriculture Organization)

Mr. Chairman, delegates to the Assembly of FAO, it is indeed an honour to be privileged to speak to this distinguished group, representing as you do so many nations, coming together as you are to advance the interest of food and agriculture around the world. It is an especial privilege to me because I was honoured to be a member of the delegation from the USA at the Quebec Conference when the charter for FAO was signed. I have a priceless treasure because it was with my fountain pen that the Chairman of our delegation signed for the United States of America. From then until now, I have watched with great interest the progress made by FAO. These six years have been years of progress. Progress in many ways. First of all, I think in a physical way it is marvelous that the country of Italy has provided this great beautiful building for the permanent use of FAO. All of us are deeply indebted to them, and I share the gratitude which I know all of you feel.

Great progress has been made in the Organization round the world. To me it is a matter of pride that such competent men and women have been selected for the work of FAO in the respective countries where the work is being carried forward so well today. Progress has been made in the programs of many areas of the earth in increasing food production. In fact, all of us together can be proud of the accomplishments of FAO, but proud as we are of the achievements up to date, all of us I know must realize that we are losing the fight of increasing food production as compared with increasing population in the world. We have had the report from the Director-General that while the population of the world has grown 12% since World War II, we have increased food production only 9%, so we must face reality that we are losing the fight and it is not necessary. We can win the fight. It can be won because we have enough scientific and technical knowledge now available, if applied, to produce sufficient food to feed adequately and well all of the teeming millions of the world.

A great group of scientists and technicians in laboratories and experiment stations around the world is continually increasing our knowledge of food production, food preservation, nutrition, and distribution of food. These advances in science and technology are not the monopoly of any nation or group of nations, but are available for the use of mankind. These advances have been made possible by the contributions of all nations in the past years, and we have borrowed from all people around the world.

In livestock, we have borrowed our great beef cattle breeds from the British Isles, our dairy cattle from the Channel Islands, Switzerland, Germany, from the Low Countries, from Scotland. We have borrowed beef cattle from India; our horses from Arabia, from the Middle East, from France, from Belgium and from Spain. We have borrowed from round the world swine, and sheep. We have borrowed our poultry from everywhere. Our foundation livestock has come from all over the world to the Western Hemisphere. Not only that, we have borrowed our wheat from Turkey—Turkey Red they call it—which has been the foundation of our great wheat production.

We have borrowed grasses from Africa; melons from Africa and the Middle East; horticulture products from all over this world; our citrus fruit from the Middle East, from Spain, Italy and Brazil. Our alfalfa from Turkey and the Middle East; our clovers from Persia and Korea. From Manchuria and from North China the great crop of soy beans which has come to be a billion dollar crop each year. In turn, the Western Hemisphere has furnished to the world potatoes; sweet potatoes, the yams, the Irish potato, and tobacco. On the other hand, the American Indian furnished sugar cane, corn, maize to all mankind.

We have borrowed scientific data. We have borrowed and used in the Western world and now we come with technical assistance. It is a two-way street. We are cooperatively sharing the advances that have been made in science, technology, genetics and nutrition. And so we come, all of us together with full knowledge that none of us has come empty-handed. Every country represented has made some contribution to the sum total of our knowledge of food and food production.

By joining hands together we can win this fight and can win it in this generation. We know enough now, if this knowledge is applied to win this fight. And so I come this morning representing the United States of America, as Administrator of President Truman's Point 4 program—the Technical Cooperation Administration—and I come offering you such facilities as we have cooperatively in food and agriculture.

Your great Director-General and I have been friends for a quarter of a century. Together we are working to bring about close cooperation in our agencies. In like fashion, we join the Colombo plan. All agencies will have to work cooperatively if we can win in this hard fight to feed all mankind. We have two great problems involved: (1) How can we find a way to live together in peace; (2) How can we produce enough to feed and clothe and house and educate mankind and bring health in like fashion to all people everywhere. We come, representing as we do our agency, hoping that you will accept us, hoping that cooperatively together we may be able to achieve more than we can separately.

I have believed in FAO since its beginning. I believe in it now—in its great leadership—and I come congratulating you on the achievements made and hoping in the years ahead through education—universal for all people—all the children of all people, girls and boys alike, through experimentation and research and through extension, that we may be able to win the fight in this struggle to feed a hungry world.

I thank you, Director Dodd, and your associates for this opportunity you have given me this morning to address this distinguished group of men and women, and all of us from America come offering you the cooperation which we are ready to share to the limit of our ability. It is our hope that from time to time many of you will find it possible to visit the United States of America and when you do, if you will let us know that you are there, you will find us ready and willing to extend to you the same courtesies which you have so generously extended to us in your respective countries when we have visited you at your homes. Thank you!

Bennett Distinguished Fellows

Oklahoma State University

Adnan Badran: President of Petra University, Jordan. He served as Jordanian Prime Minister and Minister of Defense. He serves in various organizations promoting international scientific education.

Paul W. Bass: Author of the biography, *No Little Dreams*, about Henry Garland Bennett. He also authored two other books in the Bennett Centennial Series: *Fellow Dreamers* and *Point Four: Touching the Dream*. He has also authored *Robert S. Kerr: Oklahoma's Pioneer King*.

Judge Thomas E. Bennett: Recently retired administrative law judge with the Social Security Administration. He is the youngest son of former Oklahoma A & M President Henry and Vera Bennett.

Tony Blair: Former Prime Minister of Great Britain, he is currently serving as the Quartet Representative to the Middle East helping Palestine to prepare for statehood. He has also launched the Tony Blair Faith Foundation and the Tony Blair Sports Foundation.

Dr. Lawrence L. Boger: Oklahoma State University's 14th president. He implemented many international initiatives for OSU.

Richard L. Boger: President and chief executive officer of international businesses. He worked with international interests related to chambers of commerce.

Jim Clifton: Served as CEO of Gallup, a leader in organizational consulting and public opinion research. His most recent innovation, the Gallup World Poll, is designed to give the world's 7 billion citizens a voice in virtually all key global issues.

Charles R. Eitel: Past CEO and Chairman of Simmons Bedding Company. He has been active in international business organizations.

Gibesa Ejeta: A product of the Ethiopian agricultural school projects initiated by OSU, he completed graduate studies at Purdue University. His work in sorghum hybrids earned him the 2009 World Food Prize.

Conrad and Joy Evans: Oklahoma State University faculty who served in Ethiopia assisting in educational improvements. They continue an active organization, Oklahoma-Ethiopia Society, promoting continuing relationships and providing scholarship support for Ethiopian students.

Dr. B. Dell Felder: Administrator in higher education in American institutions. She served as administrator with the Zayed University in the United Arab Emirates.

Steve Forbes: Chairman and CEO of Forbes, Inc., and Editor-in-Chief of Forbes magazine, having numerous international editions. He campaigned twice for the Republican nomination for the Presidency.

President Vicente Fox: Former President of Mexico. He led Mexican economic reform and continues to advance economic interest in Mexico.

Harriet M. Fulbright: President of the J. William & Harriet Fulbright Center. She continues the work of her late husband, Senator J. William Fulbright, in encouraging international education.

Robert Gates: Served as director of the Central Intelligence Agency and the Secretary of Defense under eight presidents. He has been awarded the Presidential Medal of Freedom, National Security Medal, the Presidential Citizens Medal, National Intelligence Distinguished Service Medal and the Distinguished Intelligence Medal.

Honorable Benjamin A. Gilman: Former congressman from New York. He worked in international relations congressional committees and as a congressional delegate to the United Nations.

James E. Halligan: Oklahoma State Senator. He was the 16th president of Oklahoma State University, expanding campuses and programs across the state.

Dr. B. Curtis Hamm: Educator initiating international education experiences for students. He serves as a consultant to Oklahoma State University to advance international studies.

Dr. James G. Hromas Past director of the International Education and Outreach and was responsible for directing the IE&O and School of International Programs at OSU.

Donald and Cathey Humphreys: Dallas residents from Tulsa, this couple has been influenced by international experiences that have "reinforced the value of learning outside one's own culture." In 2010 the Humphreys donated $6 million to support OSU's study abroad program under the School of International Studies.

Michael S. Hyatt: Financial professional for over 35 years. He currently serves as chairman of Sister Cities International and has many community membership activities.

Col. R. Alan King: Author of *Twice Armed: An American Soldier's Battle for Hearts and Minds*. He served as a military commander in Iraq with distinguished service.

Dr. Paul B. Liao: Former CEO of Tetra Tech KCM, a leading international consulting, engineering and technical services organization employing 10,000 people in over 250 offices completing projects in over 35 countries.

Dr. M. Peter McPherson: President of the National Association of State Universities and Land-Grant Colleges. He continues to encourage study abroad initiatives and programs.

Alfredo Miranda: President of UPAEP University in Puebla City, Mexico. With his strong business background, he has created innovative program of international alliances with partners such as OSU to develop intercultural competent professionals in Mexico and the United States.

Dr. Duck-Woo Nam: Former Prime Minister of the Republic of Korea. He continues his interest with many international economic organizations.

Richard Poole: Formerly served as Dean of the College of Business and OSU Vice President for University Relations. He has chaired the OSU College of Business's International Committee and helped establish the OSU School of International Studies.

Gen. Colin L. Powell: Former Secretary of State and military commander for 35 years. He serves today in promoting national education improvements and volunteerism activities.

Roger Randle: Experiences range from the Peace Corps, Oklahoma Congress and Mayor of Tulsa. His positions on Oklahoma education institutions and international boards led him to serve as the past president of the Tulsa Global Alliance.

Condoleeza Rice: Leaving a very successful career at Stanford University, she became assistant to President Bush for national security affairs and later as the 66th U. S. Secretary of State.

Ana Maria Salazar: Member of the Council on Foreign Relations. She continues to consult as a recognized export on Latin American international law and national security issues.

Dr. Robert L. Sandmeyer: Professor and Dean Emeritus of the Oklahoma State University College of Business Administration. He advised the Minister of Higher Education and Scientific Research at the United Arab Emirates University. He also authored the concept paper for the OSU School of International Studies.

Honorable Wes W. Watkins: Former congressman from Oklahoma. He obtained funding for the Wes Watkins Center and the Oklahoma Research and Technology Park, both in Stillwater, Oklahoma. He continues to promote business and agricultural development in Oklahoma.

Jack Welch: As the former CEO of General Electric Company, he has been a highly respected business speaker and author. He serves as Special Partner with the private equity firm, Jack Welch, LLC.

Dr. Clifton R. Wharton, Jr.: Educator and economist with distinguished careers in philanthropy, foreign international development, higher education, diplomacy and business. He specialized in international development in Latin America and Southeast Asia.

School of International Studies Graduates

Year	Name	State/Country
2000	Freytez, Angel	Venezuela
	Golembiewski, Andrew	California
	Trenfield, Aaron	Oklahoma
2001	Ajiboye, Kathryn	Nigeria
	Alvarez, Diego	Colombia
	Buie, Amanda	Colorado
	Castilla, Marcus	Oklahoma
	Fisher, Kevin	Oklahoma
	Fox, Stephanie	Colorado
	Konan KanKan, Omer	Ivory Coast
	Migunov, Dmitry	Russia
	Randolf, Amy	Oklahoma
2002	Allgeier-Teater, Hallie	Colorado
	Arutyunova, Angelika	Uzbekistan
	Baidildayaeva, Gulzhan	Kazakhstan
	Chastin, Catherine	Oklahoma
	Darmoe, Joseph	Ghana
	El-Assi, Shariff	Oklahoma
	Heng, Augustine	Malaysia
	Holbrook, Whitney	Oklahoma
	Inglis, Eleanor	Oklahoma
	Jeon, GiSun	South Korea
	Mancada, Gloria	Venezuela
	Schuster, Dinah	Montana
	Shook, Kalee	Oklahoma
2003	Barnes, Stuart	Oklahoma
	Brazeel, Stanna	Oklahoma
	Davila, Araceli	New Mexico
	Dugger, Jennifer	Oklahoma
	Durrani, Fiza	Pakistan
	Gallagher, John	Oklahoma

	Hueneke, Laurie	Iowa
	Kim, Daebum	South Korea
	Kwek, Siew Sim Ming Chin	Malaysia
	Lai, Mei	Taiwan
	Macharia, Angela	Kenya
	Meharg, Samuel	Missouri
	Merriman, Raquel	Texas
	Shipka, Danny	Oklahoma
	Stevenson, Michael	Montana
	Vallee, Carolle	France
	Vandrell, Jonathan	Oklahoma
	Yemenu, Abenet	Ethiopia
2004	Alagappan, Adaikappan	India
	Alemu, Asamenew	Ethiopia
	Antoku, Hitoshi	Japan
	Banihashim, Shatha	United Arab Emirates
	Beardsley, Tamara	Montana
	Christensen, Aaron	Oklahoma
	Coimbatore, Kangaraj	India
	Coley, Charles	Texas
	Cramer, Brett	Oklahoma
	Cross, Alexander	North Carolina
	Deushev, Renat	Uzbekistan
	Glenn, Brittany	Oklahoma
	Joray, Maya	Switzerland
	Kovalov, Maksym	Ukraine
	Lentz, Ben	Oklahoma
	Miller, Andrew	Oklahoma
	Nair, Ambika	India
	Noss, Christine	France
	Prentice, Benjamin	Oklahoma
	Terry, Hollee	Oklahoma
	Thrasher-Cateni, Tamara	Texas
2005	Akhtar, Muhammed	Pakistan
	Bonneyrat, Jean-Baptiste	France
	Burrows, April	Oklahoma
	Champlin, Carissa	Mississippi
	Chapin, Eric	Minnesota
	Chong, Mun Kit	Malaysia

	Fleming, Linda	Oklahoma
	Harriott, Tami	Deleware
	Henson, Matthew	Oklahoma
	Jimenez, Fernando	Mexico
	Kanjadza, Martin	Malawi
	Kumar, Shailendra	India
	Kuncova, Barboa	Czech Republic
	Lee, Thaksin	Thailand
	Machado, Karine	Brazil
	Musabaeva, Anara	Kyrgystan
	Namasivayam, Vidya	India
	Nelson-Prado, Jami	Oklahoma
	Nova, Marcela	Czech Republic
	Park, Lai Hyun	South Korea
	Pukstas, Mindaugus	Lithuania
	Sagarnaga, Jose	Mexico
	Sydorenko, Sergiy	Ukraine
	Thamsrivilai, Rungnapa	Thailand
	Vylehzhanina, Svitlana	Ukraine
	Williams, Cory	Oklahoma
2006	Abbosov, Elyor	Uzbekistan
	Abdurakhmanov, Anvar	Uzbekistan
	Arroyo, Enrico	Oklahoma
	Ephrahim, Suzzane	Tazmania
	Eshpulatov, Shahboz	Uzbekistan
	Faltynkova, Linda	Czech Republic
	Francis, La Crecia	Texas
	Garrett, Robert	Oklahoma
	Hamidov, Samir	Azerbaijan
	Jahangir, Fakhar	India
	Kolpakov, Alexander	Russia
	Meiyappan, Sudha	India
	Moore, Michael	Oklahoma
	Nabors, Craig	Oklahoma
	Park, Jinhong	South Korea
	Poteet, Sunni	Oklahoma
	Pyles, Mary	Oklahoma
	Rhodes, Erica	Missouri
	Saisi, Patrick	Kenya

	Scott, Ashleigh	Texas
	Sevene, Julieta	Mozambique
	Shahid, Parves	Pakistan
	Springer, Jennifer	Illinois
	Su, Lianfan	China
	Tran, Phong (Brian)	California
	Valtr, Casie	Oklahoma
	Vaqueiro, Ana	Venezuela
	Webb, Macey	Kansas
	Wolthuis, Samantha	New Jersey
2007	Abdeljawad, Lara	Oklahoma
	Aluri, Ajay	India
	Amin, Ahmed	Pakistan
	Cooper, Whitney	Oklahoma
	Crow, Carrie	North Carolina
	Gregory, Nicholas	Oklahoma
	Hasegawa, Hiromi	Japan
	Holbrook, Whitney	Oklahoma
	Hunter, Jason	Oklahoma
	Jannu, Deepak	India
	Jivetti, Billy	Kenya
	Jun, Jong-Ho	South Korea
	Kinsey, Julie	Oklahoma
	Lake, J. R.	Oklahoma
	Martin, Cecilia	Oklahoma
	Mirza, Ali	India
	Mohan, Mayoor	United Arab Emirates
	North, Beverly	Oklahoma
	Romero, Daniela	Mexico
	Shrewsbury, Linda	Oklahoma
	Smith, Matthew	Oklahoma
	Swift, Rebecca	Utah
	Thekijumroon, Pavine	Thailand
	Thomas, Sonia	Oklahoma
	Vasileva, Svetlana	Bulgaria
2008	Alvarez, Denise	Texas
	Bondarchuk, Yevgen	Ukraine
	Brown, Donna	Oklahoma
	Casey, Patrick	New York

	Chanjarean, Itsared	Thailand
	Choo, Hwai Jeng	Malaysia
	Domnick, Noah	Oklahoma
	Herren, Janet	Oklahoma
	Hromas, Lindy	Oklahoma
	Jenkins, Jessica	Oklahoma
	Johnson, Chandra	Minnesota
	Kim, Yongmin	South Korea
	Kratochvilova, Katerina	Czech Republic
	Krehbiel-Burton, Lenzy	Oklahoma
	Lee, Jeong-Youn	South Korea
	Lopez, Marilyn	Missouri
	Love, Daren	Oklahoma
	Mbodji, El Hadji	Senegal
	Mejia, Maria	Mexico
	Moore, Jarrod	Oklahoma
	Mutai, Daniel	Oklahoma
	Nainani, Reema	India
	Nkangama, Kerone	Malawi
	Northcutt, Katherine	Oklahoma
	Noss, Marie-Christine	France
	Roman, Alina	Romania
	Siksnelyte, Zivile	Lithuania
	Sizemore, Penny	Oklahoma
	Stallings, Monty	Oklahoma
	Stewart, Jeff	California
	Tidenberg, Laura	Oklahoma
	Tillis, Troy	Illinois
	Tshisevhe, Jeffrey	South Africa
	Van Eldon, Mark	Australia
	Velasco, Pedro	Venezuela
2009	Bardisbanian, Joe	Texas
	Burciaga, Ramon	Mexico
	Chen, Aiching	Kansas
	Devina, Tesa	Indonesia
	Egzity Erko, Netsanet	Ethiopia
	Furr, Kathleen	Oklahoma
	Garrison, Latoya	Ohio
	Gasparian, Bruno	Brazil

	Gordon, Kati	Oklahoma
	Gudero, Firew	Ethiopia
	Howard, Liz	Missouri
	McLean, Jeremy	Wyoming
	McLean, Sean	Oklahoma
	Medellin, Victoria	Texas
	Quiroz Perez, Maria	Mexico
	Roberts, Erica	Pennsylvania
	Roberts, Ronica	Oklahoma
	Sadashiva Reddy, Roopesh	India
	Sanchez, Enrique	Mexico
	Tkachenko, Iryna	Ukraine
	Wilson, Latasha	Oklahoma
2010	Abdeljawad, Loreen	Oklahoma
	Ahmed, Faez	Iraq
	Arroyo, Kate	Oklahoma
	Babayeva, Firyuza	Turkmenistan
	Blumbaha, Baiba	Latvia
	Chen, Yan Yu	Taiwan
	Deshpande, Ketaki	India
	Eleazer, James	Alaska
	Eleazer, Robin	Alaska
	Fielding, Ross	Oklahoma
	Fosnacht, Andrew	Kansas
	Gillispie, Alice	Oklahoma
	Le, Phuong	Viet Nam
	Long, Ashley	Oklahoma
	Long, Damien	Oklahoma
	Mac, Sylvia	Oklahoma
	Mack, Richard	Oklahoma
	Mitchell, Ramey	Oklahoma
	Montgomery, Julia	Arkansas
	Nuradeen, Kosar	Iraq
	Odenyo, Yolanda	Sweden
	Payne, Bryan	Oklahoma
	Prayoonwet, Wanawan	Thailand
	Saparmamedova, Jahan	Turkmenistan
	Seyoum, Negede	Ethiopia
	Schulke, Erica	Michigan

	Shinn, Allie	Oklahoma
	Simpson, Jeff	Nebraska
	Sirhindi, Amna	Pakistan
	Springer, Kyle	Oklahoma
	Steer, Deerison	Virginia
	Swadener, Hilary	Oklahoma
	Thanyajaroen, Thanakanit	Thailand
	Tkacheno, Maryna	Ukraine
	Tviska, Marta	Ukraine
	Young, Heather	Oklahoma
2011	Alemu, Michael	Ethiopia
	Arshakian, Arakssi	Iraq
	Bell, T. J.	Texas
	Chirchir, David	Kenya
	Douglas, John	Iowa
	Grayson, Erica	Oklahoma
	Hashimi, Mohammad	Afghanistan
	Kaniev, Eraj	Tajikistan
	Kovtun, Natalia	Ukraine
	Lugg, Andrew	Oklahoma
	Nedovyesov, Oleksandr	Ukraine
	Nguyen, Hieu	Viet Nam
	O'Reilly, Adrienne	Texas
	Osman, Siham	Ethiopia
	Palacios, Catalina	Mexico
	Phan, Hang	Viet Nam
	Posavec, Metaja	Croatia
	Schweitzer, Julie	France
	Shatkovskaya, Natalia	Poland
	Shita, Hiruy	Ethiopia
	Tariq, Faisal	India
	Trakalo, Ashley	Canada
	Utseshava, Katisiaryna	Belarus
	Williams, Cynthia	Florida
	Young, Ray	Oklahoma
	Zhansultanov, Rafael	Kazakhstan
2012	Abdeljawad, Juliet	Oklahoma
	Ablorh, Nadia	Oklahoma
	Bercegeay, Katie	Louisiana

Bobytskyi, Anton	Ukraine
Bondarenko, Vladislav	Ukraine
Buslaieva, Alisa	Ukraine
Campos, Aglae	Mexico
Cleary, Caitlin	Oklahoma
Delvecki, Ajax	Oklahoma
DeMissie, Michael	Ethiopia
Diaz Ramos, Geraldo	Mexico
Dicks, Kristina	Oklahoma
Elaroua, Melissa	Oklahoma
Ferguson, Jessica	Nebraska
Filkins, Lindsay	Texas
Flynn, Matthew	Oklahoma
Franzgrote, Dana	Canada
Grant, Martha	Oklahoma
Harkin, Sean	Oklahoma
Hsu, Christopher	Texas
Hunter, David (Cody)	Oklahoma
Hutchins, Matthew	Oklahoma
Isa, Kylychek	Kyrgyzstan
Johnson, Adam	Oklahoma
Khamung, Rungnapa	Thailand
Khan, Anita	Oklahoma
Kidanemariam, Rebekah	Ethiopia
Lanie, Brooke	Texas
Le, Quy	Viet Nam
Lieb, Jessica	Oklahoma
Lozano, Blanca	Mexico
McCreary, Candace	Oklahoma
Mirzayev, Kanan	Azerbaijan
Ngo, Que	Viet Nam
Nguyen, Kien	Viet Nam
Nguyen, Phuc	Viet Nam
Nilsen, Matt	Oklahoma
Pelaez, Johanna	California
Penick, Mary	Oklahoma
Porec, Samantha	Oklahoma
Rissman, Moritz	Germany
Roach, Jackson	Oklahoma

	Rojas, Lina	New York
	Shemereko, Anatoloiy	Ukraine
	Susa, Mihaela	Romania
	Tello, Rodrigo	Mexico
	Teter, Michael	Oklahoma
	Torres, Luis	Mexico
	Vazquez, Luis	Mexico
	Walters, Kelsey	Oklahoma
	Williams, Shane	Oklahoma
	Zuyonak, Natalia	Belarus
2013	Agyekum, Gabriel	Ghana
	Armstrong, Clifford	California
	Austillo, Eva (Melissa)	Mexico
	Briggs, Leslie	Oklahoma
	Canady, Curtis	Oklahoma
	ChahardahCheriki, Sara	Iran
	Condley, Matthew	Oklahoma
	Corona, Rocio	Mexico
	Dicks, Kristina	Oklahoma
	Dolan, Josephine	Oklahoma
	Dominquez, Samantha	Mexico
	Forsyth, Alyssa	Illinois
	Honea, Katie	Oklahoma
	Hudson, Stephen	Oklahoma
	Kennedy, Brandy	Texas
	Yeun Ko, Dong	Korea
	Cayton-, Van	Viet Nam
	Martinez, Orlando	Mexico
	Newland, Brandon	Oklahoma
	Nilsen, Matt	Virginia
	Nguyen, Doug	Viet Nam
	Nguyen, Mong	Viet Nam
	Ortega, Esther	Mexico
	Petrie, Nedege	New York
	Ramirez, Rodrigo	Mexico
	Rios, Marco	Mexico
	Rodriguez, Daniela	Mexico
	Ruiz, Cristina (Maria)	Mexico
	Salim, Rosalina	Indonesia

	Traslosheros, Nuria	Mexico
	Uemura, Mai	Japan
	Valencia, Miquel	Mexico
	Varqhese, Ginsey	Oklahoma
	Wilson, Christina	Oklahoma
	Winters, Andrie	Oklahoma
	Woldearegay, Bemnet	Ethiopia
	Worthy, Billy	New York
	Wu, Qi	China
2014	Andya, Fregenet	Ethiopia
	Baker-Noblot, Lindsey	Kansas
	Begashaw, Eldad	Ethiopia
	Bobos, Mihaela	Romania
	Bridgers, Audrey	Oklahoma
	Castillo Sanchez, Marcela	Mexico
	Chahardah Cheriki, Sara	Iran
	Chansriniyom, Chantaporn	Thailand
	DeLara, Christy	Oklahoma
	Dillsaver, Kate	Oklahoma
	DuVall, Bruce	Washington
	Hernandez Cortez, Mariana	Mexico
	Hernandez, Marissa	Mexico
	Herrera Medrano, Moises	Mexico
	Hiriart Lozoya, Jahaziel	Mexico
	Hudson, Stephen	Oklahoma
	Ladd, Cassidy	Oklahoma
	Ladd, Brent	Oklahoma
	Lobato Zamora, Gilberto	Mexico
	Long, Jessica	Oklahoma
	Meza Tellez, Angel Alberto	Mexico
	Mosquera Rozo, Paula	Mexico
	Nguyen, Hang	Vietnam
	Noblot, Andrew	U.S. Citizen from Morocco. No state In U.S. origin
	Sasamit, Sariya	Thailand
	Tanasap, Piyawan	Thailand
	Taormina, Jordan C.	California
	Wang, Yongshun	China

| Wehba, Cassady | Oklahoma |
| Zarate Tellez, Ana | Mexico |

2015

Almy, Alexandria	Texas
Beasley, Damon	Indiana
Clark, Kayla Christine	Oklahoma
Cooper, Tara	Oklahoma
Dozal, Claudia	Mexico
Garcia, Nohema	Mexico
Garnica Campuzano, Lina	Mexico
Honea, Katie	Oklahoma
Ibukun, Ayodeji Ayorinde	Nigeria
Kadia, Cecile	Oklahoma; But from Congo
Lu, Yi-Fang	Taiwan
Metcalf, Dawson	Oklahoma
Molleno, Catherine	Ohio
Robledo Gallegos, Miriam Olivia	Mexico
Segura Juarez, Jessica	Mexico
Teter, Sean	Oklahoma
Varela Valenzuela, Alberto	Mexico
Velasco Ortiz, Alejandro	Mexico
West, Samantha	Oklahoma

Number of Graduates each year:

2000-	3
2001-	9
2002-	13
2003-	18
2004-	21
2005-	26
2006-	29
2007-	25
2008-	35
2009-	21
2010-	36
2011-	26
2012-	52

2013-	39
2014-	30
2015-	19

Total graduates year to date   <u>353</u>

Number of Students by State		**Number of Students by Country**	
Alaska	2	Afghanistan	1
Arkansas	1	Australia	1
California	6	Azerbaijan	2
Colorado	3	Belarus	2
Delaware	1	Bolivia	1
Florida	1	Brazil	2
Illinois	3		
Indiana	1	Bulgaria	1
Iowa	2	Canada	2
Kansas	4	China	3
Louisiana	1	Colombia	1
Michigan	1	Croatia	1
Minnesota	2	Czech Republic	4
Mississippi	1	Ethiopia	13
Missouri	4	France	5
Montana	3	Germany	1
Nebraska	2	Ghana	2
New Jersey	1	Haiti	1
New Mexico	1	India	14
New York	4	Indonesia	2
North Carolina	2	Iran	2
Ohio	2	Iraq	3
Oklahoma	130	Ivory Coast	1
Pennsylvania	1	Japan	3
Texas	15	Kazahkstan	2
Utah	1	Kenya	4
Virginia	2		
Washington	1	Korea	1
Wyoming	1	Kyrgystan	2
		Latvia	1
(Total, 29 states, 199 students)		Lithuania	2
		Malawi	2

Malaysia	4
Mexico	40
Mozambique	1
Nigeria	2
Pakistan	5
Poland	1
Romania	2
Russia	2
Senegal	1
Singapore	1
South Africa	1
South Korea	8
Sweden	1
Switzerland	1
Taiwan	3
Tajikistan	1
Thailand	10
Turkmenistan	2
Ukraine	13
United Arab Emirates	2
Uzbekistan	5
Venezuela	4
Vietnam	11

**(Total, 53 countries,
203 students)**

It is reported that 2,014 international students from 102 different countries were on the Oklahoma State University campus for the Fall 2015 semester. The top five countries represented among the international student body are India, China, Saudi Arabia, South Korea, and Iran.

End Notes

Introduction

1. Email correspondence with Diego Alvarez, 2009
2. Email correspondence with Kathleen Furr, 2009
3. School of International Studies historical files, Wes Watkins Center, Oklahoma State University, 2009

Part One: Legacy and Leadership

1. Rulon, Phillip Reed. *Oklahoma State University- Since 1890*. 1975, page xiii.
2. From materials in the School of International Studies historical files, Wes Watkins Center, Oklahoma State University, 2009.
3. Oklahoma State University web site, Presidential Information, 2009.
4. Murphy, Patrick M. *Student Life and Services, Centennial Series*. Oklahoma State University, Stillwater, Oklahoma, 1988, page 51.
5. Oklahoma A & M Yearbooks, *Redskins*, 1906-07 and 1910-11, student photos.
6. Murphy. *Student Life and Services*, pages 115-116.
7. Bass, Paul William. *Henry Garland Bennett: Educator and Statesman*. New Forums Press, Stillwater, Oklahoma, 2007, pages 1-5.
8. ibid., pages 7-10.
9. ibid., pages 10-15.
10. ibid., pages 17-24.
11. Rulon. *Oklahoma State University- Since 1890*, pages 219-220.
12. Bass. *Henry Garland Bennett: Educator and Statesman*, pages 25-33.
13. ibid., pages 35-36.
14. ibid., pages 40-44.
15. ibid., pages 45-58.
16. ibid., pages 59-62.

17. Gill, Jerry Leon. *The Great Adventure: Oklahoma State University and International Education*, Oklahoma State University Press, Stillwater, Oklahoma, 1978, page 123.
18. Dollar, Doug. *OSU Alumni Association, Centennial Series*, Oklahoma State University, Stillwater, Oklahoma, 1992, pages 106-107.
19. Gill, Jerry L. *International Programs: Centennial Histories Series*. Oklahoma State University, Stillwater, Oklahoma, 1991, page 123
20. Gill. *The Great Adventure*, page 46.
21. Gill. *International Programs*, page 148.
22. ibid. page 173.
23. Bass. *Henry G. Bennett*, 2007, page 27.
24. ibid., page 34.
25. Murphy. *Student Life and Services*, page 324.
26. Peace Corps web site.

Part Two: Leadership and Learning

1. Bass. *Henry G. Bennett*, 2007, page 75.
2. Bingham. *Articles and Speeches of Henry Garland Bennett*, 1952. From an article written for The Teacher, Magazine of the Southern Baptist Convention, published posthumously February 1952.
3. ibid., Bingham
4. Gill. *International Programs*, page 148.
5. From materials in the School of International Studies historical files, Wes Watkins Center, Oklahoma State University, 2009.
6. International Student Statistics, OSU, 2009.
7. From materials in the School of International Studies historical files, Wes Watkins Center, Oklahoma State University, 2009.
8. Personal Interview with Jose Sagarnaga, OSU-Mexico Liaison Office, 2009.
9. From materials in the School of International Studies historical files, Wes Watkins Center, Oklahoma State University, 2009.
10. ibid.
11. ibid.
12. ibid.
13. ibid.
14. ibid.

15. ibid.
16. ibid., Campbell report, January 3, 1990.
17. ibid.
18. Personal interviews with Robert Sandmeyer, David Henneberry, James Osborn, Stephen Miller and James Hromas, 2009.
19. Henry G. Bennett Distinguished Fellow Award recipients, Oklahoma State University web site, Lawrence Boger.
20. Quote from Robert Sandmeyer in the Dr. Lawrence Boger Distinguished Professorship brochure.
21. Henry G. Bennett Distinguished Fellow Award recipient, Oklahoma State University, October, 2007
22. School of International Studies Dedication Program, 1999, program personalities, Oklahoma State University, David Henneberry.
23. ibid., James Osborn.
24. ibid., Stephen Miller.
25. Walton S. Bittner Service Citation information, James Hromas, 2009.
26. Henry G. Bennett Distinguished Fellow Award recipient, Oklahoma State
    University, October, 2013
27. Richard Poole materials provided by Jim Shideler, 2009.
28. From materials in the School of International Studies historical files, Wes Watkins Center, Oklahoma State University, 2009, Administrative   Committee.
29. ibid., Curriculum Committee.
30. Henry G. Bennett Distinguished Fellow Award recipients, Oklahoma State
    University web site, James Halligan.
31. Personal interview with James Halligan, 2009.
32. From materials in the School of International Studies historical files, Wes Watkins Center, Oklahoma State University, 2009.
33. ibid.
34. Chart information from the international student services offices.
35. Personal interview with James Halligan and James Hromas, OSU, 2009.
36. Personal interview with James Hromas, OSU, 2009.

37. From materials in the School of International Studies historical files, Wes Watkins Center, Oklahoma State University, 2009.
38. ibid.
39. *SIS Dedication Program*, Oklahoma State University, April 1, 1999, page 24.
40. ibid.
41. ibid.
42. ibid.
43. Personal interview with Kay Keyes, 2009.
44. Email correspondence with Diego Alvarez, 2009
45. Correspondence with Kevin Fisher, 2009.
46. From materials in the School of International Studies historical files, Wes Watkins Center, Oklahoma State University, 2009.
47. Personal interview with Tim Huff, 2009.
48. Correspondence with Bryan Pardee, 2009.
49. Correspondence with Blake Lowry, 2009.
50. Correspondence with Gemma Hughes, 2009.
51. Correspondence with Laureen C. Manners, 2009.
52. Correspondence with Nana Honda, 2009.
53. Correspondence with Anne-Charlotte Sequeval, 2009.
54. Correspondence with Benjamin Prentice, 2009.
55. Correspondence with Brian Tran, 2009.
56. Correspondence with Bryan and Katie Thomason, 2009.
57. Bass. *Henry G. Bennett*, 2007, page 75.
58. Personal interview with Vera Preston-Jaeger, 2007
59. FY09 Annual Report, Peace Corps.
60. Correspondence with Cajuan Theard, 2009.
61. Correspondence with Noah and Liz Domnick, 2009.
62. Correspondence with Samantha Wolthuis, 2009.
63. FY09 Annual Report, Study Abroad.
64. ibid.
65. ibid.
66. Correspondence with Andrew Golembiewski, 2009.
67. Correspondence with Gi-son Jeon, 2009.
68. Correspondence with Matthew Henson, 2009.
69. Correspondence with Stephanie Fox, 2009.
70. Correspondence with Stuart Barnes, 2009.
71. Correspondence with Elsa Velasco, 2009.
72. Correspondence with Ajay Aluri, 2009.

73. Personal interview with Donna Birchler, 2009
74. Personal Interview and correspondence with Conrad Evans, 2009.
75. OSU International Education and Outreach FY09 Annual Report, Oklahoma State University, 2009, Introduction.
76. FY09 Annual Report, International Outreach Unit.
77. Correspondence with Eleanor Inglis, 2009.
78. Correspondence with Fernando Jiminez-Arevalo, 2009.
79. FY09 Annual Report, Fulbright Resource Center, 2009.
80. ibid.
81. FY09 Annual Report, Phi Beta Delta Honor Society. 2009.
82. List of OSU-International Commitments, 1999-2009, Graduate Program office, 2009.
83. The First Five Years, 1999-2004, School of International Studies, Oklahoma State University, April 8, 2004, Stillwater, Oklahoma.
84. Tenth Anniversary Celebration, School of International Studies, Oklahoma State University, April 9, 2009, Stillwater, Oklahoma
85. Personal interview with James Hromas, 2009.
86. From materials in the School of International Studies historical files, Wes Watkins Center, Oklahoma State University, 2009.
87. ibid.
88. ibid.
89. ibid.
90. ibid.
91. ibid.
92. Henry G. Bennett Distinguished Fellow Award recipients, Oklahoma State University web site, B. Curtis Hamm.
93. FY09 Annual Report, Graduate Program.
94. Personal Interview with Gerry Auel, 2009.
95. From materials in the School of International Studies historical files, Wes Watkins Center, Oklahoma State University, 2009.
96. Tenth Anniversary Celebration, School of International Studies, Oklahoma State University, April 9, 2009, Stillwater, Oklahoma.

Part Three: Learning and Looking Ahead

1. Correspondence with Dr. David Henneberry, November 2013.
2. International Studies and Outreach newsletter, Issue 2, Winter 2013.
3. Correspondence with Jeff Simpson, November, 2013 and January 2015.
4. ibid.
5. ibid.
6. ibid.
7. ibid.
8. International Studies and Outreach newsletter, Issue 11, Fall 2012.
9. Correspondence with Dr, Joel Jenswold, November 2013 and January 2015.
10. ibid.
11. Correspondence with Kay Keyes, December 2013.
12. Correspondence with Steve Hallgren, November 2013.
13. ibid.
14. Correspondence with Dr. David Henneberry, November 2013.
15. International Studies and Outreach newsletter, Issue 5, Spring 2012.
16. Correspondence with Marissa Hernandez, November 2013.
17. Correspondence with Rodrigo Tello, November 2013 and January 2015.
18. ibid.
19. Correspondence with Dr. David Henneberry, November 2013.
20. Correspondence with Jim Shideler, November 2013.
21. Correspondence with Anthony Cambas, November 2013 and January 2015.
22. ibid.
23. Correspondence with Katie Reim Sewell, November 2013.

Conclusion and Appendix:

1. Correspondence with Robert Garrett, 2009.
2. Oklahoma State University web site, 2009.
3. Bigham, Jonathan. *Speeches and Articles by the Late Dr. Henry Garland Bennett as Administrator, Technical Cooperation*

Administration, Department of State. TCA Public Affairs Office, U. S. Department of State, 1952.
4. Oklahoma State University web site, International Studies and Outreach, Bennett Distinguished Fellows, 2009.
5. Statistics provided by the Academic Programs Office of the School of International Studies.

Resources

Books:

Arrington, Michael, and Downs, Bill. *Once in a Hundred Years.* Marceline, Missouri, 1985.

Bass, Paul William. *No Little Dreams: Henry Garland Bennett, Educator and Statesman.* New Forums Press, Stillwater, Oklahoma, 2007.

Bass, Paul William. *Fellow Dreamers: Oklahoma Education and the World.* New Forums Press, Stillwater, Oklahoma, 2008.

Bass, Paul William. *Point Four: Touching the Dream.* New Forums Press, Stillwater, Oklahoma, 2009.

Bingham, Jonathan. *Shirt Sleeve Diplomacy.* John Day Company, New York, 1953.

Bigham, Jonathan. *Speeches and Articles by the Late Dr. Henry Garland Bennett as Administrator, Technical Cooperation Administration, Department of State.* TCA Public Affairs Office, U. S. Department of State, 1952.

Boggs, James H. *Governance, Centennial Histories Series,* Stillwater, Oklahoma: Oklahoma State University, 1992.

Dollar, Doug. *OSU Alumni Association, Centennial Histories Series.* Oklahoma State University, 1992.

Fite, Robert C. *Extension and Outreach, Centennial Histories Series.* Oklahoma State University, 1988.

Gill, Jerry Leon. *The Great Adventure: Oklahoma State University and*

International Education. 1978.

Gill, Jerry L. *International Programs, Centennial Histories Series.* Oklahoma
State University, 1991.

Murphy, Patrick. *Student Life and Services.* Centennial Series, Oklahoma State
University, 1988.

Peters, David C. *The Campus of OAMC.* New Forums Press, Still-water,
Oklahoma, 2009.

Rulon, Philip Reed. *Oklahoma State University—Since 1890.* Okla-homa State
University, 1975.

Warne, William, E. *Mission for Peace: Point 4 in Iran.* IBEX Publishers,
Bethesda, Maryland, 1956, 1999.

Publications:

"Dedication Proceedings," School of International Studies, Oklahoma State University, April, 1999, Stillwater, Oklahoma

"The First Five Years, 1999-2004," School of International Studies, Oklahoma State University, April 8, 2004, Stillwater, Oklahoma

"Tenth Anniversary Celebration," School of International Studies, Oklahoma State University, April 9, 2009, Stillwater, Oklahoma

"International Education & Outreach, Celebrating 10 years in 2009, Advancing OSU's 60-year international legacy, School of International Studies," Oklahoma State University, Stillwater, Oklahoma

"OSU International Education and Outreach FY09 Annual Report," Oklahoma State University, 2009

International Studies and Outreach newsletters, 2012-2013

Interviews and Correspondence: (22)

Aeul, Gerry, July 7, 2009
Birchler, Donna, July 7, 2009
Dollar, Doug. June 22 and June 24, 2009, Stillwater, Oklahoma

Evans, Conrad. June 23, 2009, Stillwater, Oklahoma
Gill, Jerry, July 7, 2009 and
Halligan, James. July 22, 2009
Hanneberry, David, July 9, 2009
Hargis, Burns, September 8, 2009
Hernandez, Marrissa, November, 2013
Hromas, James, June 25 and July xx, 2009, Stillwater, Oklahoma
Huff, Tim, July 9, 2009
Jenswold, Joel, November, 2013
Keyes, Kay, July 7, 2009
Miller, Stephen, July 7, 2009
Osborne, Jim, July 23, 2009
Sandmeyer, Robert, September 10, 2009, Stillwater, Oklahoma
Simpson, Jeff, November, 2013
Telwahade, Mel, 2011-2013
Tello, Rodrigo, November, 2013
Voss, Kevin, July 9, 2009
Watkins, Wes, September 8, 2009
Wilkinson, Nancy, July 22, 2009

Graduate Survey/Questionnaire Information: (38)

Alemu, Negede S.
Aluri, A. J.
Alvarez, Diego
Barnes, Steve
Black, Evan
Clemo, Matt
Darmoe, Joseph
Domnick, Noah
Fisher, Kevin
Fox, Stephanie
Furr, Kathleen (Kat)
Garrett, Robert
Golembiewski, Andrew
Gonzalez, Alejandra
Hannah, Alex
Henson, Matt

Hling, Hling
Honda, Nana
Hughes, Gemma
Inglis, Eleanor
Jeon, Gi-sum
Jimenez, Fernando
Jivetti, Billy
Kanjadza, Martin H.
Lenckner, Christian
Lowry, Blake
Manners, Lauren C.
Metcalf, Dawson
Pardee, Ryan
Prentice, Benjamin
Sequeval, Anne-Charlotte
Serrano, Luis
Theard, Cajuan
Thomason, Bryan and Katie
Tran, Brian
Velasco, Elsa
Wolthuis, Samantha
Worthy, Billy

Index

Burciaga, Ramon 116
Burkina Faso 37, 71, 75
Buslaieva, Alisa 119
Buthod, Kyle 72

C

California 44, 48, 112, 115, 116, 119,
    121, 123
Calzadillas, Vernise 83, 85
Cambas, Anthony xvii, 90, 92, 130
Cameroon 89
Campbell, John R. 29, 104, 127
Campos, Aglae 119
Canada 3, 42, 56, 68, 89, 118, 119,
    123
Canady, Curtis 120
Lotven, Ann 33
Cantwell, James W. 104
Cayton, Van 120
Center for International Trade Devel-
    opment (CITD) xv, xvi, 27, 29,
    37, 47, 59, 73, 90, 91, 143
ChahardahCheriki, Sara 120, 121
Chen, Aiching 117
Chen, Yan Yu 117
Chile 21, 34, 69, 71
China ix, x
Chirchir, David 116
Clark, Barry 37
Cleary, Caitlin 79, 119
Clemo, Matt 69, 135
Clifton, Jim xvi, 91, 108, 111
Colombia xi, 39, 56, 75, 112, 123
Colorado 112, 123
Condley, Matthew 120
Congo 75, 89, 122
Connell, James Henry 104
Connell, Vera (Bennett) 5
Corona, Rocio 120
Cosmopolitan Club 3
Costa Rica 31, 56, 80, 89
Couto, Felipe 57
Croatia 118, 123
Czech Republic 56, 70, 75, 89, 114,
    116, 123

D

Damron, Joshua 79
Darnell, Danny 101
Delvecki, Ajax 119
DeMissie, Michael 119
Deleware 123
Denmark 56, 87
Deshpande, Ketaki 117
Devina, Tesa 116
Diaz Ramos, Geraldo 119
Dicks, Kristina 119, 120
Dicks, Mike 90
Diop, Abdoulaye 57
Dollar, Doug and Gayla 102, 126, 134
Dolan, Josephine 120
Dominican Republic 46
Dominquez, Samantha 120
Domnick, Noah and Liz 46, 101, 116,
    128, 135
Douglas, John 118
Dunnigan, Nikkie 101
Durant, Oklahoma 5
Dust Bowl 16

E

Ecuador 34, 45, 75
Egypt xv, 3, 8, 56
Egzity Erko, Netsanet 116
Eitel, Charles R. 108
Ejeta, Gibesa 108
Elaroua, Melissa 119
Eleazer, James 117
Eleazer, Robin 117
England ix, 6, 21, 42, 56, 89
England, Taylor 88
English Language Institute (ELI) xv,
    xvii, 2, 14, 38, 40, 44, 65, 69,
    74, 76, 85, 94, 99
Eskridge, James E. 88, 104
Estonia 89
Ethiopia xv, xvii, 7, 9, 12, 14, 17, 22,
    34, 52, 56, 57, 60, 66, 75, 89,
    91, 93, 108, 109, 113, 116, 119,
    121, 123
Evans, Conrad and Joy 14, 19, 22, 37,
    109, 129, 135

T

U

About the Authors

Paul William Bass was born in Independence, Missouri. He was the oldest of six boys. He graduated from William Chrisman High School; Southwest Baptist College in Bolivar, Missouri; and Midwestern Baptist Theological Seminary in Kansas City, Missouri. He married Janet Sue Smashey in 1969. He served in full-time church staff positions in Arkansas, Alabama and Missouri. In 1990 he accepted a staff position at Ouachita Baptist University in Arkadelphia, Arkansas. While on staff he served in bi-vocational church positions in Arkansas. He served at Ouachita as Director of Student Activities and Summer Conferences, adjunct instructor and intercollegiate debate coach. He retired in 2007 and began his writing career. In 2012, he and Jan retired to Willard, Missouri.

Books that Bass has authored and awards he has received include the following:

No Little Dreams, Henry Garland Bennett: Educator and Statesman, 2007 Henry G. Bennett Distinguished Fellow Award, Oklahoma State University, 2007

Fellow Dreamers: Oklahoma, Education and the World, 2008

Point Four: Touching the Dream, 2009

In Jesus' Names, 2010

Minor Characters of the Bible, 2010

Robert S. Kerr: Oklahoma's Pioneer King, 2012, Missouri Writer's Guild First Place President's Award, 2013 Walter Williams Major Work Award, 2013

Grace through Tolerance, 2014

Me and Church, 2015

A History of Fort Leonard Wood, Missouri, 2016, Acclaim Press: Sikeston, Missouri

The books are available from NewForumsPress.com and Amazon.com. The author can be contacted at bassp@obu.edu.

Katie Reim Sewell works for the Division of International Studies and Outreach at Oklahoma State University. She serves as the Marketing and Events Coordinator.

Katie grew up on a farm near Billings, Oklahoma and went to college at Oklahoma State University. She received her bachelor's and master's degrees in Agricultural Communications. Katie went to work for Agricultural Communications Services at OSU after graduation and worked there for seven years before taking her current position.

She married Jason Sewell in 2013 and together they have two children, Jack Henry and a baby girl due in April 2016.

Katie enjoys traveling, reading, running, yoga, OSU sporting events, and spending time with her family.

She can be contacted at Katie.Sewell@OKstate.edu.

www.ingramcontent.com/pod-product-compliance
Lightning Source LLC
Chambersburg PA
CBHW071444090426
42737CB00011B/1773